POLITICAL PORTRAITS

GENERAL EDITOR
KENNETH O. MORGAN

Jawaharlal
NEHRU

DENIS JUDD

GPC Books is an imprint of the University of Wales Press,
6 Gwennyth Street, Cardiff, CF2 4YD.

First published 1993

© Denis Judd, 1993

British Library Cataloguing-in-Publication Data
A catalogue record for this book is available from the British Library
ISBN 0-7083-1171-7
ISBN 0-7083-1175-X pbk

All rights reserved. No part of this publication may be reproduced, stored in a retrieval system, or transmitted, in any form or by any means, electronic, mechanical, photocopying, recording, or otherwise, without the prior permission of the publishers.

The right of Denis Judd to be identified as author of this work has been asserted by him in accordance with the Copyright, Designs and Patents Act, 1988.

Cover design: T. C. Evans, Acen

Typeset in Wales by Megaron, Cardiff
Printed in England at The Bath Press, Avon

Contents

		page
Editor's Foreword		vii
Preface		xi
1	The Silver Spoon: Origins, 1889–1912	1
2	Apprentice Congressman, 1912–1921	7
3	Socialist, Satyagrahi and Internationalist: the 1920s	12
4	The 1930s	20
5	The Second World War, 1939–1945	30
6	The Last, Slow Steps to Freedom, 1945–1947	42
7	Partition and Freedom, 1947–1948	50
8	Prime Minister, 1948–1956	57
9	Final Years and Mounting Problems, 1956–1964	69
10	Nehru's Legacy	83
Notes		87
Bibliography		89
Index		93

Editor's Foreword

The aim of this open-ended series of short biographies is to offer personal portraits of several of the decisive figures in the making of British politics over the past two hundred years. It will range over leading practitioners of politics, from Britain and Ireland (and indeed the commonwealth/empire as well) who have vitally shaped our public affairs in the nineteenth and twentieth centuries. Its premise, of course, is that people and biographies are vitally important as explanatory keys to the past. Too often, historians tend to see the course of historical change in terms of vague impersonal factors, evolutionary patters, underlying themes, even that Scylla and Charybdis of historical understanding, 'forces' and 'trends'. The impact of the disciplines of economics, sociology or anthropology is often taken as reinforcing this tendency, and helping to obliterate flesh-and-blood human beings from our map of the past.

Now, no one would seriously dispute the enrichment of historical studies that has resulted from the stimulus of other disciplines. At the same time, it can hardly be questioned that the role of key individuals, locally and regionally as well as nationally, has been crucial in shaping the rhythms and speed of our political development in the years since the twin impact of industrialization and representative democracy. The growth of our political parties is impossible to visualize without the personal imprint of Gladstone, Disraeli or Keir Hardie. The course of wars, and their consequences, would have been totally different if Lloyd George or Churchill had never lived. Without Parnell or de Valera, modern Ireland would not have emerged in its present form. Even in the 1980s, the dominance of Mrs Thatcher confirmed anew the powerful impulses that can be realeased by the authority or whim of one determined individual.

So there need be no apology for offering a new series of biographies, brief but authoritative, all written by expert scholars, designed for the intelligent general reader as well as for the student or the specialist, as launch-pads for political and historical understanding. Portraits of individuals, naturally, open up wider social, cultural or intellectual themes. They also help to make history fun – vibrant, vivid, accessible. They may also be a means to a deeper understanding of our world. It should always be remembered that Karl Marx himself, whose influence is so frequently taken as eliminating individuals entirely from history in favour of the rise and conflict of social classes, actually took the reverse view himself. 'History', Marx wrote, 'is nothing but the activity of men in pursuit of their ends. Some of these men – and women – and the ends they pursued, achieved, missed out on, or simply forgot, are illustrated in this series.

Jawaharlal Nehru, whose career is assessed here by Denis Judd, a specialist on imperial history, was one of the outstanding figures in the emergence of Third World nationalism and the downfall of empire. The product of an exclusive and privileged upbringing, he was foremost among the young Indian intellectuals stirred by Gandhi's call for national resistance to the Raj just after the First World War. He was a paradoxical figure in many ways – an aristocratic leader of a mass popular uprising, a state socialist who endorsed Gandhi's appeal to rural simplicity, a rationalist who responded to Hindu mysticism, the anti-British product of Harrow and Trinity. But by the Second World War, he was evidently Gandhi's and the Congress's main political voice, his authority reinforced by years in British gaols. He played a crucial role in the negotiations with successive British viceroys, and with the Muslim League. They saw the transfer of power to free India in August 1947, but also a partitioned subcontinent and mass communal carnage. He then served as India's prime minister throughout the early phase of independence. As Denis Judd shows, the years down to 1956 were marked both by impressive internal reform and a growing international eminence, with Pandit Nehru's leadership the lynchpin of the new Indian democracy. Thereafter came a period of growing difficulty, with increasing political and communal strain, economic failures and a loss of authority worldwide, following military humiliation by the Chinese. The situation was fluid and precarious at the time of Nehru's death.

Anyone who has visited modern India must be impressed by the ambiguity of Nehru's legacy. India has become a remarkable experiment in mass democracy, in contrast to neighbouring Pakistan and Burma, and a leading voice in Asian and world affairs. It is greatly modernized and its caste system in decline. At the same time, this democracy has rested on the dynasticism of the Nehrus and has been punctuated by the assassination of leaders and frequent communal and religious violence. The social and economic advance of India has been chequered, with massive poverty and illiteracy, sectarian conflict and an uncontrollable explosion in the population, especially evident in the capital, New Delhi. Nehru's burial monument alongside the Jumna arouses a variety of emotions amongst modern Indians. Denis Judd does not conceal these tensions, nor the complexity of his personal relations with Gandhi, Cripps and Mountbatten amongst others. But he also sets out Nehru's courage, strength and idealism in grappling with immense difficulties, and his stature as a maker of our world.

KENNETH O. MORGAN
University of Wales, Aberystwyth

Preface

I am very grateful to all those who have helped me in the writing of this book. Dr John Campbell gave me early encouragement. So did Bruce Hunter, who played a vital role in the success of the whole enterprise, and who was assisted throughout by the proficient and constructive Kate Lyall Grant. The University of North London gave me valuable research relief, and my students, especially those taking various South Asian history units, were both a stimulation and a challenge. Dr Howard Brasted sent support from the Antipodes.

I owe an enormous debt of gratitude to the Series Editor, Professor Kenneth Morgan, not only for his enthusiasm for the book, but also for reading the text so carefully and for making so many valuable suggestions for its improvement. Naturally, in the time-honoured way, I take responsibility for any remaining flaws. I have also been greatly impressed by the friendly efficiency of the editorial staff at the University of Wales Press, notably Susan Jenkins and Liz Powell. Their task was undoubtedly made easier by having a text that had been so expertly typed by April Morris. My parents, my wife Dorothy, and, in varying degrees, our four children, all lent support to the project.

DENIS JUDD
London, 1992

1
The Silver Spoon: Origins, 1889–1912

Jawaharlal Nehru was one of the foremost founders of modern India, second only to Mahatma Gandhi himself. Unlike Gandhi, however, Nehru was born relatively great although, during a lengthy life, he also achieved greatness and was willing, even eager, to have greatness thrust upon him.

The third born, but only surviving, son of Motilal Nehru, the joint head of a wealthy and politically sophisticated Kashmiri Brahmin family that had finally settled in Allahabad, Nehru was also a product of Harrow School and Cambridge University. He was at first overshadowed by his father Motilal, a Congress party stalwart who early on saw the potential of Gandhi's *satyagraha* (or truth-force) tactics as a means of mobilizing the Indian masses in the struggle to rid the sub-continent of British rule.

By the mid-1920s Jawaharlal Nehru, declaring his faith in the newly established Bolshevik regime in Russia, was a leading light of the reconstructed and revitalized Indian nationalist movement. He developed a close political and personal relationship with Gandhi, despite their fundamental disagreements over the merits of socialism and the relevance of western culture and materialism to the Indian experience. The two men were profoundly and consciously complementary to each other, and Nehru saw Gandhi as a father-figure, particularly after the death of Motilal Nehru in 1931.

Jawaharlal Nehru played a vital role in promoting the cause of Congress and all-India unity in the years leading to independence in 1947. He was prepared to pay a high price, including frequent imprisonment and harassment, for his principles, although it must be said that, for all its high-handedness and occasional acts of brutality, the British Raj was no Third Reich.

When India finally achieved self-rule, 'at the midnight hour', Nehru became the first Prime Minister of the new, though partitioned, nation. He was already a statesman of international standing, and his stature was to increase in a post-war world where imperialism was in retreat before the forces of nationalism. Nehru presided over India's attempt to establish its international identity and to cope with its domestic tensions and inadequacies. At the same time he became a symbol of stability and sanity among the world's leaders. Despite the conflict with Pakistan and China, despite the intractable nature of many of India's domestic problems, Nehru was a leader whose position was not seriously challenged at home or abroad. He became a father figure of the new, multi-racial Commonwealth – quizzical, philosophical and shrewd. When he spoke upon the world stage it was not to rant and posture but to address great issues with a calm maturity.

Few could deny Nehru's adroit political skills, nor his personal charm – to which the last Vicereine Lady Mountbatten, among others, apparently succumbed. Yet it is arguable whether he left India a more prosperous or progressive country at his death, even though he had set in train forces for long-term social, political and economic change. The Five Year Plans, the Community Development Projects, the legal abolition of Untouchability, the new Hindu Code, the attacks on the caste system, were examples of his zest for modernization and progress. Yet much remained the same.

Overseas he pursued a rigorous (though not too rigorous) policy of non-alignment – a curious stance for one so firmly wedded to many western values. He became a *de facto* spokesman for new and relatively under-privileged nations everywhere. He gave India a distinctive identity in world affairs, but could not make her a truly great power. Nehru was idolized at home and respected abroad. Not the least of his achievements was to bequeath a dynastic succession to a nation that believed passionately in democracy. Whether this apparent paradox is simply part of a wider and more dangerous confusion over his perceived and his real accomplishments will be considered in due course.

Jawaharlal Nehru was born on 14 November 1889 at Allahabad. The Nehrus were comparative newcomers to the region known after 1901 as the United Provinces. The family had originally been part of the Kashmiri Pandit community. These antecedents gave the Nehru family certain distinctive qualities as compared with other Hindus of the United Provinces. Although the Pandits of Kashmir were well aware of their high status, inter-caste prejudices were not deeply entrenched in their lives. Among the Hindus of Kashmir there were no castes below that of Brahmin, nor was there a great deal of feeling of separateness from, or antagonism towards, the Muslim majority of that province. It is worth noticing that Motilal was more fluent in Arabic, Persian and Urdu than in any other language. Motilal's own father had died three months before his birth, but his two older brothers had ensured that he had received a proper education in the English language, and eventually he entered the Law, becoming one of the leaders of the Bar in Allahabad.

Motilal was an outward-going, confident man, to whom legal and financial success came easily. Like many members of the educated Indian élite he became involved in the activities of the Indian National Congress, though at the same time virtually living the life of a brown-skinned English gentleman.[1]

Jawaharlal Nehru was brought up amid luxury and privilege. The family had a private swimming pool and tennis court, and the boy was surrounded by all the trappings of affluence. It has been argued that his mother's influence ensured a sufficiently intense experience of Hindu custom and folklore, despite the fact that Motilal was no docile practitioner of the religion, having been excommunicated in 1899 for his refusal to make atonement for travelling overseas.

It is also significant that Motilal used his wealth to buy the best that British education could offer to his eldest son. There were English governesses, a brief time at a local convent, and finally a protracted period of private instruction at home. Perhaps the most profound influence upon Jawaharlal came from the young theosophist, F. T. Brooks, between 1901 and 1904. Brooks introduced Jawaharlal to British poetry and literature and, by setting up a small laboratory in his rooms, also provoked an interest in science. It is arguable that, by being exposed to theosophy, with its intense, individualistic approach to religious experience, the young Nehru came to develop a scepticism towards the miraculous properties of orthodox faiths.

In May 1905, Motilal took the momentous decision of taking his family to Britain and sending his son to Harrow School. Jawaharlal was now a slightly built, strikingly handsome boy of fifteen years. As the family began their journey back to India, Motilal wrote to his son:

> In you we are leaving the dearest treasure we have in this world, and perhaps in other worlds to come. We are suffering the pangs of separation from you simply for your own good... I think I can without vanity say that I am the founder of the fortunes of the Nehru family. I look upon you, my dear son, as the man who will build upon the foundations I have laid and have the

satisfaction at seeing a noble structure of renown rearing up its head to the skies.[2]

Father and son were to maintain a vigorous correspondence. Motilal soon wanted to know the smallest details: 'Give me a complete account of your first fagging day. I am so anxious to know what menial services are exacted at Harrow from the only and dearly beloved son of a man who employs more than 50 servants in India.' Jawaharlal replied: 'Besides lighting fires and carrying messages I have to turn on toshes [school slang for bath or footpan] for sixth formers after footer.' Overall, Jawaharlal did all the things required of a dutiful public schoolboy, playing football and cricket, running in cross-country steeplechases, skating, supporting his house in various competitions, and excelling academically. At the end of the first term he was able to inform his father, 'I was of course top of my form and I am told that a prize will be given to me. I never thought of this happening and am rather nervous about it.' A few months later however, he was indicating that he was finding his experience at Harrow both limiting and boring, telling his father: 'I must confess I cannot mix properly with English boys. My tastes and inclinations are quite different. Here boys, older than me and in higher forms than me, take great interest in things which appear to me childish . . . I almost wish sometimes that I had not come to Harrow, but gone straight to the 'Varsity.'[3]

Quite apart from any local difficulties, events in the world outside would have encouraged Jawaharlal's growing disillusionment with his environment. The 1905 partition of Bengal by the Viceroy, Lord Curzon, had unleashed some of the most serious anti-British agitation since the Mutiny. The Congress movement, which had been founded in 1885 (only four years before Nehru's birth) as a means for Indians to express, mostly discreetly, their criticisms of British rule, was given a fresh impetus by the Bengal partition. Partly as a result, Congress became increasingly polarized between the moderates, led by G. K. Gokhale, who believed in constitutional reform, and the extremists who were pressing for stronger measures in opposition to the British Raj. Jawaharlal followed these developments keenly, asking his father to send him Indian newspapers regularly. Not merely was Indian nationalism beginning to assert itself in a more businesslike fashion, but Nehru's arrival in Britain had more or less coincided with Japan's crushing defeat of Imperial Russia in a far-eastern war which had destroyed almost at a stroke the assumption that western powers were invariably superior to those of Asia.

In 1907 Jawaharlal sat the entrance examinations to Cambridge University, going up to Trinity College in the October of that year. In the summer before he went up to Cambridge, he spent a few weeks in Ireland. There he identified with the cause of Irish nationalism, and was particularly impressed by the Sinn Fein movement. This was a time when the active nationalists of both India and Ireland were inclined to identify with each other as allies in a common struggle against British imperialism. At any rate, Nehru found his increasingly extremist and nationalist sympathies strengthened by his Irish experience, to the extent that he accused his father of being 'immoderately moderate'.[4] There is some evidence that Motilal Nehru was upset by this and similar radical posturing by his son.

He need not have worried. Jawaharlal did not get involved in student politics at Cambridge, and his extremist opinions seem to have been more of a deliberately cultivated dilettantism than the expression of some profound political philosophy. He showed himself to be quite prepared to accept his father's ambitions on his behalf that he should on his return to India enter the Indian Civil Service. It is surprising, in view of Nehru's later political career, that he seems to have viewed the prospect of such a fate with equanimity. In the event, it was Motilal who abandoned the idea of a career in the Indian Civil Service for his son in 1910, and then mainly because he did not relish the prospect of Jawaharlal serving for lengthy periods in remote districts far from home. He was also, incidentally, convinced that the examiners were increasingly biased against Indian candidates.

There is generally the impression that Nehru's Cambridge days were spent in a half-hearted fashion, mainly in the pursuit of pleasure. He does, however, seem to have become deeply interested in the writings of William Morris, buying a full set of his collected works in 1910. Morris, of course, was identified with an eloquent and consistent attack on class exploitation and the brutalizing effects of industrial capitalism. William Morris became, if anything, more revolutionary and progressive as his life developed, and, although there was to be no conscious imitation, Jawaharlal Nehru's life was to develop in a similar fashion.

Nehru seems to have been in no need of close intimate social relationships while at Cambridge. It is true that he had many acquaintances, and his sporting activities (he was made cox of the Trinity Boat Club) brought him into contact with quite a large number of his fellow undergraduates, but the overriding impression is of a somewhat solitary, egoistic hedonism.

Before he took his final tripos examinations, Jawaharlal had joined the Inner Temple, encouraging his father to believe that his son would make, like him, a brilliant career at the Law. But the plain fact was that Nehru had no great enthusiasm for the Law. This lackadaisical attitude had been reflected in his final university tripos examinations which had placed him in the second half of the second class. For two years after graduating, Nehru enjoyed life in London. He was very much the man of fashion, but found it difficult to manage money effectively and frequently approached his father for financial help. One of his biographers has said of him that 'he never in his life had any money sense.'[5]

Back in India, Motilal was becoming increasingly perturbed by his son's lack of progress. Jawaharlal merely managed to pass the Bar examinations; there was no distinction or the winning of scholarships. It was if he was simply marking time in order to placate and gratify the father for whom he had so much affection. In 1912, Motilal brought his son back to India. He was given a rapturous reception by his family and was soon earning his first fee, the substantial one of 500 rupees as a lawyer – a commission that he owed to his father's reputation rather than to his own abilities. Few would have predicted a brilliant career for this handsome, graceful, sensitive but apparently aimless young man. As it happened, his varied cosmopolitan experiences in Britain were to provide the fertile soil for a great personal and political flowering.

2
Apprentice Congressman
1912–1921

For the first four years after his return to India, Jawaharlal lived the conventional, privileged life of the well-to-do professional middle class of Allahabad. Membership of his father's chambers brought him plenty of legal work and useful social contacts, but did not fill him with enthusiasm; he found the Law tedious, and was often inhibited when pleading. More to his taste were the personal pleasures and luxurious lifestyle that, as a bachelor, Allahabad offered him. In February 1916, however, he married. Motilal and his wife had been giving thought to the choice of a bride for their son ever since Jawaharlal had gone to Harrow. Still the dutiful son, Jawaharlal was content to let his father settle his engagement. In 1912, Motilal chose a young girl of thirteen who belonged to a Kashmiri Brahmin middle-class family, very similar to his own. Kamala Kaul had been educated at home and spoke Hindi and Urdu. When she reached the age of seventeen her marriage to Jawaharlal was celebrated in Delhi on a grand and opulent scale.

It is not easy to assess what Nehru's marriage meant to him. Although it produced, in 1917, one inordinately loved child, their daughter Indira, the future Prime Minister of India, it was not otherwise prolific. A prematurely born son died in 1924, and three years later there was a miscarriage. In the early years of her marriage, Kamala had to bear the disapproval of some of her husband's family who considered her social origins inferior to their own. She was, moreover, frequently ill, and the tuberculosis that was first diagnosed in 1919 finally brought her to an early death in 1936. Kamala was often depressed, and there is no doubt that her husband's superior intellectual and educational status, not to speak of his attractiveness to other women, put the marriage under considerable stress, particularly during its early years. Despite the periods of neglect by her husband,

Kamala eventually grew in self-confidence, and apparently found her protracted illness an impetus to value life more and to become involved, however modestly, in the struggle for Indian freedom.[1] In 1931 she was even arrested and went to prison for her activities, an event which not merely demonstrated her own growing self-confidence but also helped to bring her closer to her husband.

In 1917 Jawaharlal gave one of the clearest expressions so far of his political commitment by joining the Home Rule League set up in the United Provinces, with his father as president and himself as one of the joint secretaries. The establishment of a number of Home Rule Leagues throughout India was primarily the work of the theosophist Mrs Annie Besant, who passionately supported Indian self-determination, and the militant nationalist B. G. Tilak. The establishment of the Home Rule Leagues was partly a response to the failure of Congress to readmit the extreme element which it had previously ejected, but also partly a move to educate politically, through the holding of meetings and seminars, the organization of social work, and the circulation of literature. The Government of India's harassment of Mrs Besant (she was finally interned at a hill station by the Madras government in 1917) seems to have been the final goad that drove Jawaharlal into joining his local Home Rule League, though his earlier theosophist education may also have been a factor.

Despite this show of political commitment, Nehru still gave the impression of a man who had yet to think through his nationalist attitudes. Was he an extremist, or in fact, as sometimes appeared, more of a moderate? Even though in 1919 he helped to run *The Independent*, a newspaper established by his father to give some expression to Congress attitudes in the United Provinces, he seems not to have found it particularly fulfilling. What he needed was a means of focusing his somewhat nebulous views and of galvanizing his energies. The events of 1919 and the inspired leadership of M. K. Gandhi were to provide him with that purpose and inspiration. There is a strong case for viewing the year 1919 as one of the great turning-points in the history of Indian nationalism. It was a year when both the worst and the best aspects of the British Raj were openly displayed, and when literally millions of Indians became finally disillusioned with their rulers.

The fair face of British imperialism was shown in the great reforms mainly encapsulated in the Government of India Act of 1919. Known as the Montagu–Chelmsford reforms, after the current Secretary of State for India, Edwin Montagu, and the Viceroy, Lord Chelmsford, these measures built on the Morley–Minto reforms of a decade earlier, and also were seen as a reward for the invaluable and generally staunch loyalty that India had shown for the allied cause during the First World War. The Montagu–Chelmsford reforms apparently made sweeping concessions to Indian nationalist demands. The main points were as follows. The Viceroy's Executive Council should now consist of four British and three Indian members. There would be a majority of elected Indian representatives on the Central Legislative Council, and big Indian majorities in the provincial parliaments. It was equally significant that ministerial posts in the provincial governments were to be divided between Indians and British. Although, in practice, Indian ministers were given the 'safer' jobs, those that involved hardly any threat to continuing British supremacy, they were at least now able to hold substantial office in their own land. This system of diarchy, or dual rule, might have been the foundation from which India could have advanced peacefully to dominion status within the British Empire, as Canada, Australia, and the other self-governing colonies had done.

But, like Doctor Jekyll, the British Raj could also demonstrate the brutalities of Mr Hyde. The year had opened with strong Indian objections to the implementation of the Rowlatt Acts, which essentially enabled the authorities to deal in arbitrary and summary fashion with political agitation. Gandhi made a bid for all-India leadership by calling for a national *satyagraha*, or campaign of civil disobedience, against the Rowlatt Acts. There was a patchy response to Gandhi's campaign. Then in the spring of 1919 there came the massacre at Amritsar in the Punjab, where the rigidly self-controlled Brigadier-General Dyer, faced with civil disorder, and enraged by reports of assaults on Europeans, ordered his troops to open fire without warning on a large but peaceful Sikh crowd that not only had inadequate means of dispersal but actually found gates locked against them. Over four hundred Indians died in the bloodbath. Nehru, though shocked at the massacre, was even more horrified at the subsequent reaction in Britain to the Punjab tragedy. Even though Dyer was dismissed from the army for his part in the atrocity, the House of Lords passed a motion in his favour and over £20,000 was raised on his behalf by public subscription. Sections of British opinion thought he had been harshly treated and turned their anger on the Lloyd George Government. The expressions of support that General Dyer received and the overall failure, as so many Indian nationalists perceived it, to punish him for his actions, were of crucial importance in Nehru's political evolution. Despite his flirtations with Indian nationalist extremism, Jawaharlal had been more comfortable in the mainstream of the Indian moderate tradition. After

Amritsar he now realized that freedom could never be guaranteed as a gift but could only be achieved through a determined and comprehensive struggle.

In the aftermath of Amritsar, Nehru threw in his lot with Gandhi. But the Gandhian programme of non-cooperation involved the boycotting of elections to the new councils and the rejection of office. Motilal Nehru disapproved of this degree of non-cooperation, and even had his eye on a suitable constituency for his son in the forthcoming council elections. Jawaharlal's rejection of his father's preferred course led to some tension between them, and the father found little pleasure in observing his son embrace the rigours of the puritanical Gandhian lifestyle. Of course, the younger Nehru could be accused of wanting it both ways; to become an austere *satyagrahi*, but one sustained by his father's affluence. At any rate, Jawaharlal now became a committed Gandhian activist. It was almost in the nature of a religious conversion. But what most appealed to Nehru was Gandhi's resolution, his overwhelming commitment to achieving political freedom for India. Although he displayed many contemplative, spiritual qualities, Gandhi was essentially a man of action, ceaselessly involved, energetic, with a great drive to control and shape events. It is significant that he frequently asserted that God appears not in person but in action. Jawaharlal was also, no doubt, attracted by Gandhi's other-worldly qualities and his steadfast rejection of the pleasures of the flesh and the indulgence of the senses. In this respect, their partnership had some of the interdependence of the attraction of opposites.

Nehru gave practical expression to his new political commitments by becoming involved, during 1920, in the peasant unrest in the United Provinces. The troubles were centred in Avadh (Oudh) and arose from the bitter conflict between impoverished tenants and extortionist landlords and middlemen. In June 1920 some five hundred protesters from Pratapgarh arrived in Allahabad hoping to meet Gandhi. Although Gandhi was not there, Jawaharlal was. The protesters persuaded him to return with the Pratapgarh, thus, almost by chance, drawing Nehru into the perennial problems of the Indian peasantry. He became actively involved in the agrarian agitations. As a Gandhian disciple he strove to link the protests of the tenants to the wider non-cooperation movement.

Early in 1921 Jawaharlal had considerable practical experience of the brutal confrontation between the United Provinces peasantry and the authorities. After a violent and bloody episode in the Rae Bareli district, Nehru, obviously deeply moved, wrote this dispatch for *The Independent*: 'They behaved as brave men, calm and unruffled in the face of danger. I do not know how they felt but I know what my feelings were. For a moment my blood was up, non-violence was almost forgotten – but for a moment only. The thought of the great leader, who by God's goodness has been sent to lead us to victory, came to me . . .'[2] Even though horrified by the violent reactions of the authorities, Nehru was eventually able to adhere to the Gandhian principles of non-violent confrontation. Perhaps he tended also to glamorize the protesters, seeing them as a sturdy and uncorrupted peasantry who could emerge as the driving force behind a successful, nationwide independence movement.

There is little evidence at this time that Nehru had considered at all scrupulously whether the great political changes that he sought should be accompanied by appropriate economic and social transformation. It seems clear that he was focused primarily upon the objective of ending British rule and, with it, British control over national finance and law and order. He had not yet embraced socialism, and looked in a somewhat sentimentalized fashion to a future in which a peaceful evolution, involving the granting of considerable powers to local village councils, held the key to future development. Exactly how rural, and indeed urban, poverty was to be ameliorated did not apparently concern him particularly deeply. Nor, despite his increasingly active political involvement, had Nehru been arrested, or imprisoned, like so many of those to whom he gave support. In the event, he was able to assuage his conscience and to court danger more provocatively by turning from local politics to all-India affairs.

3

Socialist, Satyagrahi and Internationalist: the 1920s

During the spring of 1921, Nehru, by now committed to an all-India political offensive, threw himself into promoting the non-cooperation campaign throughout the United Provinces. He undertook a strenuous tour of the various districts, speaking on behalf of both the Congress and the Muslim Khilafat movements. The transformation from the luxury-loving, comparatively idle Jawaharlal of earlier years is nicely illustrated by his willingness once, while campaigning, to run between two places at which he was to speak.[1] The results from this vigorous politicking, however, were disappointing, and the non-cooperation movement failed to gather sufficient steam in the United Provinces.

The extent of Nehru's conversion to Gandhian politics is illustrated by his new and passionate commitment to *swadeshi*, the wearing and use of home-made cloth. In the city of Allahabad he even went round door-to-door collecting foreign clothes which were later ceremonially burnt. He argued, both privately and at political conferences, that the achievement of self-rule, or *swaraj*, for India depended on the use of *swadeshi* cloth. The symbolism behind this campaign was obvious, although its effectiveness was less so. If British goods were driven from India, the British themselves would be bound to follow.

Although Nehru was generally prepared to obey various orders of the government, such as not proceeding with meetings which were specifically prohibited, the authorities in the UP were preparing to take measures against him. The attack was to be two-pronged: action would be taken against the Nehru-inspired journal, *The Independent*, for its articles, and against Jawaharlal for the making of seditious speeches. A game of cat and mouse ensued. The authorities gave both Nehrus, father and son, and the editor and printer of *The Independent*, the opportunity to commit themselves to avoiding such provocation in the future. Jawaharlal defiantly denied the accuracy of the police reporting of his allegedly seditious speeches, and refused to offer any apology or undertaking. The central Government shied away from a confrontation and decided that, for the time being, he should not be prosecuted. By November 1921, however, the Government of India decided to strike against the non-cooperation campaign and in particular to declare unlawful the volunteer organizations in the United Provinces. In December, Motilal and Jawaharlal were arrested for their official positions on the UP volunteer board.

Father and son went to prison in a mood approaching exultation. After all, how more effectively could they demonstrate their commitment to the freedom movement? Declining the privileged conditions which the jail superintendent offered them, both continued to supervise and encourage the work of Congress in the UP as best they could. Jawaharlal was released from prison, having served half his sentence, in March 1922. This early release may well have been part of the Government's response to Gandhi's calling off the civil disobedience campaign because of the increasing incidents of violence. Despite his disappointment with the ending of the all-Indian *satyagraha*, Jawaharlal returned, with even greater commitment, to the organization of homespinning, the boycotting of foreign goods, and picketing, in the United Provinces.

In May 1922, Nehru was again arrested on a charge of organizing picketing. True to the principles of non-cooperation he refused to plead in court, but instead made a lengthy statement accusing the authorities of intimidation and terrorism and emphasizing the peaceful nature of his own activities. He attacked the British Raj, and made a passionate and moving declaration of support for Gandhi:

> Jail has indeed become heaven for us, a holy place of pilgrimage since our saintly and beloved leader was sentenced ... I marvel at my good fortune. To serve India in the battle of freedom is honour enough. To serve her under a leader like Mahatma Gandhi is doubly fortunate. But to suffer for the dear country! What greater good fortune could befall an Indian, unless it be death for the cause for the full realisation of our glorious dream.[2]

Nehru had hoped for a longer jail sentence than his first, and he was not disappointed. He was sent to Lucknow District jail for eighteen months' imprisonment. The conditions under which he served his sentence were not, it must be said, too onerous. There was no hard labour; instead he was able to undertake daily physical exercise and to carry out spinning. He also read a great deal, and wrote letters suffused with his contentment with a life of, as he saw it, sacrifice and hardship. He was released from prison in January

1923, before he had served his full sentence, as part of a general amnesty declared by the United Provinces' Government. He emerged into the outside world to find the Congress movement at odds with itself. Gandhi was still in prison, and the movement's leadership was split on the issue of whether to abandon non-cooperation by entering and participating in the system of provincial and central councils. Jawaharlal was in two minds about council entry, and for a time he tried to promote a truce between the council entryists and non-entryists. He made his first impact at a national political level at the meeting of the All India Congress Committee at Bombay in May 1923. What he proposed was essentially a fudge, but it was finally agreed that the party executive should be composed of those uncommitted to either side in the council entry struggle, men such as Jawaharlal himself.

But this compromise was without substance. In July the AICC voted narrowly against Nehru's resolution calling for disciplinary action against those provincial Congress committees that had defied the compromise. Jawaharlal and his supporters resigned from the working committee as a result, and a month later he resigned as secretary of the UP provincial Congress committee as well.[3] What was Nehru to do with his new-found, comparative freedom? His trip in September 1923 to Delhi for a special meeting of Congress provided the answer. While in Delhi he heard of the crisis in the small princely state of Nabha in the Punjab. The deposition of the ruler of Nabha, for alleged maladministration, was fiercely resented by the local Sikh population, whose unrest merged with the growing strength of the Akali movement. The Akali Dahl was a quasi-military organization which had been formed to evict the frequently corrupt Hindu managers of the Sikh shrines and also to assert a generalized challenge to the Government.

Jawaharlal saw in the disturbances in Nabha the opportunity both for Congress and for the non-cooperation movement in general to exploit Sikh discontent. Nehru's entrance into Nabha State provoked a heavy reaction from the authorities. His presence was deemed unwelcome. The British administrator, now in charge of the state, had Jawaharlal and his companions arrested, handcuffed and eventually locked up in Nabha jail. After confused, and often farcical, legal proceedings, Nehru and his two companions were each sentenced to thirty months' imprisonment, but these sentences were to be suspended—on the directions of the Government of India. They were also ordered to leave the state and not to return. Although he did not test the challenge not to return to Nabha, Jawaharlal arrived back in Allahabad to a hero's welcome.

With the national non-cooperation campaign temporarily suspended, and Gandhi still in jail, Nehru tried to keep alive the ideals of direct action and peaceful revolution. As he put it: 'The choice for us is between Lenin and Mussolini on the one side and Gandhi on the other. Can there be any doubt as to who represents the soul of India today?' In September 1924, having been released from prison in February, Gandhi began a 21-day fast. Recoiling from this 'shattering news whose consequences are terrible to contemplate', Nehru threw himself into a campaign to promote national unity and to end communal discord and violence. During this brief crisis while Gandhi continued with his fast, Nehru went down with fever. An all-parties' conference in January 1925 did little to restore Nehru's faith in communal co-operation, and he seems for a while to have despaired of effectively carrying on the campaign against the Raj.

He had other troubles to contend with. In November 1924 he and his wife had lost a child after a premature birth, and shortly afterwards Kamala showed clearer signs of tuberculosis. In March 1925, Jawaharlal himself underwent a minor operation. He also found his relations with his father badly strained through his commitment to Gandhian politics. One of the problems in the father–son relationship was that Jawaharlal was embarrassingly dependent upon his father for money. Gandhi sought for ways of boosting Nehru's income, and, perhaps as a result of Motilal's intervention, the giant industrial firm of Tata offered to employ him. Unwilling to serve such capitalist masters, Jawaharlal returned reluctantly to the Law and to a lucrative brief secured for him by his father.

Nehru's political administrative experience was greatly strengthened during this time of his life by his becoming chairman of the Allahabad municipal board between April 1923 and April 1925. Although he protested that his new position was essentially a diversion from the struggle for *swaraj* (he decided to continue as secretary of the provincial Congress committee) his new post gave him his first real experience of official administration. Many of the traits which were later to be associated with his premiership surfaced during his chairmanship of the Allahabad municipal board – a tendency to dominate colleagues, a push for efficiency, a desire to advance on several fronts with new ideas and reforms, and an abiding loyalty to those who had worked efficiently for him. His achievements were necessarily limited by the scale of the problems he faced, but it was acknowledged, even by the local commissioner, that the administration of the city had been substantially improved. One small triumph for Nehru, particularly in view of his continuing commitment to Gandhian politics, was that spinning and weaving were introduced into the school curriculum.

In March 1926 Nehru set out with his wife and daughter for a lengthy trip to Europe. The main purpose of the journey was to enable Kamala to spend several months in Switzerland, in the hope that this would enable her to halt the spread of her tuberculosis. But Nehru also planned to spend time in travel and study, and his daughter Indira was to go to school, learn French and generally extend her education. At one level, it was doubtless a relief to escape from the confusion and disarray apparent within the Indian nationalist movement.

Towards the end of 1926, with his wife very little improved, the family began further travels around Europe. These journeyings brought Nehru into contact with a very wide range of European politicians, thinkers and activists. The European experience also provided what came to be regarded as a turning point in Jawaharlal's development, when he helped to organize, and indeed represented the Indian National Congress at, the International Congress against Colonial Oppression and Imperialism held in Brussels in February 1927. His experiences at this conference not merely brought him into contact with the Marxist and socialist ideas of many delegates, but also helped him to see the Indian problem within a wider context. In his statements to the press and in his speeches, Nehru went out of his way to paint a far broader-brushed picture of the Indian national struggle, placing it within the framework of the capitalist and imperialist needs of the British rulers. The conference concluded with the issuing of a manifesto, condemning European capitalism and imperialism, which owed a great deal to Marxist–Leninist theory. Although Nehru apparently took no active part in drafting the manifesto, he raised no particular objection to its contents. In fact he had by now adopted a broadly Marxist viewpoint, agreeing that capitalism and imperialism were inextricably linked together and that both would have to be eliminated.

Jawaharlal was appointed honorary president of the League against Imperialism and for National Independence. During the remainder of his stay in Europe he attended the meetings of the executive committee of the League as frequently as he could. His Marxist sympathies were, however, somewhat vague. He objected to the activities of the minority of Communists on the League's executive committee although he voiced his objections not to the socialist theory of the state but to 'being led by the nose by the Russians or anybody else'.[4]

Despite these strictures, Nehru was clearly increasingly obsessed and fascinated by the Soviet Russian experiment. In the autumn of 1927, after Motilal arrived from India, father and son were invited to the anniversary celebrations of the 1917 Russian revolution. Although the trip only lasted a few days, it made a deep impression upon Jawaharlal. He was perhaps fortunate in visiting the Soviet Union at a stage, three years after Lenin's death, when it was easy to see the remarkable reforms and improvements that had been effected in Soviet society. Stalin was establishing his supremacy, but his worst oppressions lay in the future. Jawaharlal became convinced that Russia, a primarily agricultural country with a large and illiterate population, had a great deal to teach India. He was able to savour the still self-evident idealism of the world's first major socialist state. This, together with the Marxism he had absorbed at the Brussels conference, made him highly sympathetic to Communism.

Nehru returned to India committed to the principles of revolutionary radicalism and determined that the example set by Lenin and his followers should become part of the sub-continental experience. This did not mean that he whole-heartedly rejected Gandhian politics, but he now achieved a certain independence from the Mahatma's influence. It is perhaps worth noting that this conversion was born not of the Indian experience, but from Nehru's protracted stay in Europe, where after all he had received the bulk of his early education. On his return to India, Nehru began to argue forcibly that Congress should commit itself firmly to the goal of true independence. Dominion status, recently favourably defined at the 1926 Imperial Conference in London, now seemed less attractive to him with its implication of a major continuing connection between Britain and her Dominions. He also believed that once the nationalist movement made full independence its aim, it would become less defeatist and would re-emerge as a revitalized mass movement.

Jawaharlal, therefore, armed with his new radical ideas, was all for a determined assault upon the fabric of British rule. One of the main obstacles to this new initiative was, of course, Gandhi. To Gandhi and many of his followers, Nehru seemed to be proceeding too fast and too rashly. For a while it seemed possible that there would be a serious rift between the two men, but in the end Jawaharlal drew back from the brink. Nehru continued to argue in public repeatedly against the acceptance of dominion status, even though that now meant open disagreement with his father as well as with Gandhi. Partly to propagate his ideas he now organized an Independence for India League as a pressure group within the Congress. He also advocated a modest beginning to a grand design of establishing socialism throughout India, starting in the United Provinces with the abolition of landlordism and the socialization of the land. He also argued that the state should gradually acquire key industries, guarantee a minimum living wage, increase the level of direct taxation, and put a tax on agricultural income.

This programme raised the spectre of class struggle, and of intensified conflict between industrialists and workers and between landlords and tenants. Jawaharlal was now prepared to admit that violent conflict might be necessary to resolve some of these problems, and that the final goal of the struggle might well be the establishment of some sort of communist or socialist state. Despite the passion of Nehru's advocacy it did not bring about the transformation in the Congress movement that he desired. Full-blooded socialism did not sweep through the movement, and there is evidence that some people joined the Independence for India League merely to block and divert its activities. Nehru's disappointment at his failure to refashion the Congress movement in a more socialist and revolutionary image was tempered by the finding of a cause that renewed the need for nationalist action. The appointment of the all-British Simon Commission to review the workings of the reforms of 1919 was seen as a gross affront to Indian susceptibilities, even though it contained members as sympathetic as Clement Attlee. Jawaharlal became deeply involved in the hostility to the Simon Commission and the demonstrations against it.

In December 1928 the commission arrived at Lucknow in the United Provinces. Nehru, in leading a large demonstration against the commission, was one of hundreds of demonstrators who were beaten and trampled to the ground by mounted police. The injuries that Nehru sustained greatly increased his popularity throughout the sub-continent, and Gandhi wrote to him: 'My love to you. It was all done bravely. You have braver things to do. May God spare you for many a long year to come and make you his chosen instrument for freeing India from the yoke.'[5] Doctrinal differences, however, remained. The 1928 Nehru Report, prepared by Motilal not Jawaharlal, came down heavily on the side of accepting dominion status. Congress eventually gave its support to the Nehru Report, despite Jawaharlal's evident disapproval. However he carried on with his duties as General Secretary of the Congress, putting a great deal of his energy into the promotion of volunteer corps, youth leagues and student organizations.

Towards the end of 1929, after much politicking by Gandhi and Motilal, Jawaharlal was somewhat reluctantly elected to the presidency of Congress at its next session at Lahore in December. Although there were fears that his presidency would merely serve to split the movement, by the time Congress met at Lahore the mood of most of the delegates was more closely attuned to Nehru's own policy of defiance and struggle. In his presidential address, Nehru attempted to put the problem of Indian nationalism within its international context. Furthermore, he faced delegates with the awkward fact that Indian society was deliberately based upon the principle of inequality. He also insisted that nationalism could have only one goal – complete independence from British control. Nehru went so far as to proclaim: 'I must frankly confess that I am a Socialist and a Republican, and am no believer in Kings and Princes, or in the order which produces the modern kings of industry, who have even greater power over the lives and fortunes of men than even the kings of old, and whose methods are as predatory as those of the old feudal aristocracy.'[6] Acknowledging that Congress was unlikely immediately to adopt a fully-fledged socialist programme, Nehru asserted that this was the path India would have to take if she wanted to rid herself of poverty, inequality and degradation. At the very least, he asked Congress to commit itself to ending the domination of any one class or group over another. He also advocated, in the long term, workers' control of industry on a co-operative basis and a system of peasant proprietorship. Finally, Jawaharlal returned to the main preoccupation of the Congress, the achievement of power. Here he reasserted the value of non-cooperation, strengthened by political and economic boycotts and by the withdrawal of contact with the British authorities as much as possible. There should be non-payment of taxes and general strikes. The country must be freed from foreign rule.

What did Nehru's presidential address really mean? There was no doubting his determination to rid the sub-continent of British rule. On the other hand, the socialism which he proposed was of a tentative and futuristic variety. Although he was able to place before his audience the dilemmas that faced them, particularly in the areas of social reform, he was unable to provide any immediate, effective solutions. In essence, what Nehru was trying to do was to stick to principle and to appeal to political idealists while at the same time reassuring the moderate, and often well-to-do, supporters of the Congress movement. At the very least Congress now had in its chair a leader of great intellectual capacity, glamour, and apparent integrity. If Nehru was able to remind Congress over the next ten years of the importance of the economic and social issues that faced it, he was also seen by many as the best available defence against Bolshevism and open class warfare.

4
The 1930s

As the 1930s began, the Indian nationalist cause seemed in urgent need of revitalization. The British Raj seemed to hold all the trump cards. It had been able to arrest leaders of the nationalist movement at will, and, despite *satygraha* and non-cooperation, the administration still continued to function with relative efficiency. The vast bulk of the population continued in their struggle for subsistence within the confines of a capitalist dominated and still overwhelmingly agricultural economy. The Simon Commission had carried out its enquiries, despite vehement nationalist opposition, and published its report in June 1930. With the Army and the Civil Service loyal, and with the nationalists positively striving to avoid violent revolutionary upheaval, there seemed no reason why the British authorities should not continue to control India's destinies almost indefinitely.

In fact, although British rule was to last for nearly two more decades, and although the Conservative party contained elements (headed most vociferously by Winston Churchill) that attempted to obstruct the transfer of power, there is little doubt that astute contemporary observers realized that the Raj was drawing to its close. The great reforms of 1919 were the essential springboard from which genuine self-rule could be achieved. The year 1919 was significant in one other respect; from that time onwards recruitment of British applicants into the prestigious and well-paid Indian Civil Service fell off dramatically. For the young men looking to their future careers, the writing was clearly on the wall. Well within their lifetime India would be an independent nation. Despite, or perhaps because of, British successes during the 1920s in largely neutralizing Gandhi, containing nationalism and working, none too subtly, to foment Hindu–Muslim rivalry and distrust, the authorities were plainly making way for the inevitable transfer of power. In 1924 the Royal Commission on Indianization had recommended that the Indian Civil Service should be half Indian within fifteen years, and the police force half Indian within twenty-five years. Two years earlier, the Viceroy, Lord Reading, had sent the recommendations of a report to the home government that had proposed that the Indian Army, with the exception of the Gurkhas 'should be completely Indianised in three distinct stages beginning in 1925. If all went smoothly, the Indian army would be completely controlled by Indians by 1955'.[1] Although the British Government rejected this time-scale, these various moves all indicated the underlying seriousness of British intent. Of course, Indianization of the Civil Service was made more urgent by the falling off in the number of recruits from Britain; nonetheless all the signs were there that India would, at some unspecified future date, achieve independence.

The advent of the minority second Labour Government under Ramsay MacDonald in 1929 held out the promise of further progress. In particular, the Government wished the imminent constitutional conference on India's future, which was to be held in London, to be a success. The MacDonald Cabinet effectively repudiated the Simon Commission, and went out of its way to reconcile Indian nationalist leaders to the principle of negotiated constitutional progress.

An extraordinary episode ensued. Gandhi and both Motilal and Jawaharlal Nehru were in prison. Shortly before his arrest, Motilal, who had always clung to the hope of constitutional progress through agreement and negotiation, had indicated to the authorities that there was still a possibility of a genuine accord if the impending London conference were empowered to construct a constitution which gave the substance of independence. The Raj, through various mediators, began negotiations with the jailed Congress leaders. Perhaps their eagerness to do a deal had other causes. At the start of 1930 Gandhi had made a very successful bid to recapture the political initiative, by launching a civil disobedience campaign which centred upon the deliberate breaking of the Government's salt monopoly. Jawaharlal had marched with Gandhi to Dandi to collect and manufacture salt in defiance of Government regulations. Nehru later movingly described his political mentor on this great enterprise: 'the picture that is dominant and most significant is as I saw him marching, staff in hand, to Dandi on the Salt March in 1930. He was the pilgrim on his quest of truth, quiet, peaceful, determined and fearless, who had continued a quiet pilgrimage regardless of consequences.'[2]

The British authorities went so far as to arrange a special train to take both Nehrus across the country to talk with Gandhi in Yeravda jail. Other Congress leaders joined them, and for three days what was in effect a conference of the party's high command took place, a meeting connived at by the Government whose authority they were campaigning to destroy and replace. Small wonder that Churchill, at home, denounced the Government of India, having imprisoned Gandhi, for 'sitting outside his cell door begging him to help them out of their difficulties.'[3] Churchill need not have worried: despite Gandhi's more placatory mood, the Congress leadership could not agree upon policy.

Shortly after these discussions, the Government released Motilal, who was clearly a dying man. In early October Jawaharlal, having served his sentence, was set free. After a brief, and apparently idyllic, holiday at the hill station of Mussoorie with his father, wife, daughter and other relations, he was soon back in the business of hurling political defiance at the authorities. In October an order was served on Nehru forbidding him to address public meetings. Having flouted the ban, he was arrested on 19 October 1930, brought to trial, and convicted. The sentence was the heaviest so far, two years and four extra months in prison for refusal to pay a fine. Nehru's imprisonment did something to revive the flagging civil disobedience campaign, and even inspired the fatally ill Motilal to rise from his sick bed and call for nationwide demonstrations. Some five thousand people were arrested at meetings held on Jawaharlal's birthday, and shortly afterwards his wife, Kamala, also received her first and raptuously greeted prison sentence.

Simultaneously, in London the first of the Round Table Conferences had begun. Although the delegates had in many cases been carefully selected by the British authorities, and although the Princes and other special-interest groups were all represented, with the notable exception of Congress who boycotted the proceedings, the Government was not guaranteed an easy ride. The delegates were unanimous in demanding the realization of responsible government for India. Essentially, of course, both sides agreed upon this principle, the only problem being when and how to implement the grant of self-government. In order to guarantee that at the next session of the Round Table Conference further progress should be made, the Government proceeded to make various concessions to Congress points of view. It indicated its readiness to concede full provincial autonomy and to hasten the introduction of responsible government at the centre. The Viceroy, Lord Irwin, wished to made a bid for closer co-operation with Gandhi. An Anglo-Catholic, as apparently deeply committed to Christianity as Gandhi was to his beliefs, Irwin attempted to introduce a spirit of compromise and to put 'the seal of friendship once again upon the relations of the two people, whom unhappy circumstances have latterly estranged'. To give substance to these sentiments, Irwin released Gandhi and other Congress leaders in January 1931. Despite protests in Britain, this move was clearly meant to reinstate Gandhi and the more moderate elements in Congress for the next stage of negotiations.

Jawaharlal was troubled by Gandhi's inclination to accept that there had indeed been a change of heart on the part of the British. But, for the moment, he was obliged to lay aside his objections and attend to his dying father. In February 1931, Motilal Nehru died so peacefully that his son, who was watching at the bedside, thought he was merely asleep. After Motilal's cremation on the banks of the Ganges, Jawaharlal recalled: 'The stars were out and shining brightly when we returned lonely and desolate.'

Despite the very deep attachment between father and son, Motilal's death must have represented something of a liberation for Jawaharlal. His father's controlling and dominating influence was now removed, and he could instead transfer to the equally dominating personality of Gandhi much of the affection which he had hitherto reserved exclusively for his father. The deepening and strengthening of the interdependent relationship between Nehru and Gandhi was to provide an alliance which was one of the bedrocks upon which the Indian nationalist movement was increasingly based. Motilal's death must have been liberating in another way. At one level, it symbolized for Nehru the failure and end of the old moderate Congress constitutional line. Jawaharlal was now able, without the risk of incurring parental displeasure, to press for more radical and more socialist solutions to India's problems.

The cause of moderation and compromise was not, however, dead. Indeed it lived on in Gandhi. In March 1931 Gandhi and Irwin came to the agreement which in effect accepted the constitutional position as perceived by the British Government and confirmed at the first Round Table Conference in exchange for various political amnesties, an end to oppressive police measures, the end of the salt monopoly, and other concessions.

Jawaharlal, as President of Congress, was shocked at the apparent capitulation of the Irwin–Gandhi Pact. But the Mahatma convinced him that it was a necessary expedient, and that there had been no real surrender nor any humiliation of Indian nationalism. The Pact had the appearance of an agreement between equally weighty parties and also carried the implication that Congress spoke for the majority of the Indian people. The extent of right-wing Tory rage in Britain indicates that it was hardly the capitulation which Nehru and other Indian radicals originally feared. At least the agreement established a firm basis for Congress co-operation with the British authorities.

The Pact was confirmed to a special session of Congress at Karachi in the spring of 1931. Nehru once more raised objections to the whole principle, but Gandhi once more persuaded him out of his opposition. Nehru's surrender was rewarded with Gandhi's approval of a resolution on Fundamental Rights and Economic and Social Changes. The resolution was hardly a full-blooded commitment to socialism, and indeed would not have been passed by Congress if it had been. Its implementation, also, would have to wait until independence, if then. However, it did buy off the radicals, and after independence enabled the Congress Government to claim respectable, if vague, socialist antecedents.

Gandhi, but not Nehru, attended the second session of the Round Table Conference in London in November 1931. Circumstances were perhaps not so propitious as for the first session: Lord Irwin had been replaced as Viceroy by the far less approachable Lord Willingdon; radical nationalists in India were showing their impatience at the implementation of the 1931 pact between Government and Congress; and, in the United Kingdom, the Labour administration had fallen to be replaced by a National Government – which although also led by Ramsay MacDonald was bitterly opposed by the Labour party and was effectively under the control of the Conservative majority in the Commons. Although agreeing in principle to a federated independent India, the conference got bogged down on the issue of the representation of different communities and minorities. Gandhi, who made a considerable impression on certain sections of the British public, proclaimed that Congress would accept any solution agreeable to Hindus, Muslims, and Sikhs, but he resolutely opposed the creation of separate electorates for other groups, especially for the Untouchables who, he insisted, were part of the Hindu community. Gandhi's somewhat high-handed demeanour at the second Round Table Conference served to antagonize some of the other delegates.

In India the apparent lack of progress at the conference in London did little to raise morale among the Congress leadership, which was struggling to salvage what it could of the now collapsing Gandhi–Irwin Pact. Advice was sought from Gandhi in Britain, who replied, 'Do as you think fit.' The Government of India, under the increasingly tough leadership of the new Viceroy, Willingdon, was determined to exploit differences between the different communities and, if possible, to break Congress in the process. At the end of the year when Nehru went to Bombay to meet Gandhi on his return from the London conference he was arrested. It was his sixth term of imprisonment. Gandhi, perhaps not yet appreciating that Willingdon was a very different Viceroy from Irwin, asked for a meeting to discuss the deteriorating situation. The Viceroy replied that he would only meet Gandhi on the condition that there would be no discussion of the recently introduced security ordinances or of the arrests. Gandhi then threatened a resumption of the civil disobedience movement unless Willingdon agreed to more open-ended talks. But the administration perceived Gandhi as a broken leader of a failing movement, and the Viceroy refused to meet the Mahatma 'under threat'.

Scenting the possibility of inflicting a grievous wound on Congress and, indeed, upon the whole nationalist movement, on 4 January 1932 the Government took a series of efficiently executed and unexpected measures. Gandhi and other Congress leaders were arrested immediately, to be followed over the next few months by some 80,000 other party workers. Six days later Congress was declared an illegal organization. Nehru was put on trial at Allahabad on the same day that Gandhi was taken into custody. He was sentenced to two years' imprisonment, and his two sisters were each sentenced to one year in prison. Heavy fines were imposed on a number of well-to-do Congress supporters in the clear hope that such action would lead businessmen and others to reconsider continuing their support for the movement.

These were dark days for the nationalist movement. Especially for Congress, whose leadership had been arrested and whose strategy was in tatters. Those like Nehru who had never believed in the efficacy of the Gandhi–Irwin Pact were hardly comforted by having been proved to be right. By the middle of 1932 government repression had reduced Congress to near ruin, its buildings seized, its funds confiscated, its records destroyed. The Government had imposed an uneasy, potentially threatening peace upon the country.

During the next four years Nehru spent much of the time in prison. Although his health was for a while adversely affected, he was generally treated courteously by his gaolers, and continued to take a lively interest in events in the outside world. These years saw the rise of fascism in Europe, including Hitler's seizure of power in Germany in 1933, and, nearer home, the aggressive expansion of Japan into Manchuria and beyond. The Great Depression of the early 1930s had disrupted the social and economic structures in many western democracies, which helped to confirm Nehru's belief that socialism held the key to the future. He was also convinced that there was bound soon to be a struggle to the death between the forces of fascism and communism.

He had more pressing and personal anxieties nearer home. These were the years when his wife's health finally failed and she approached her premature death. Gandhi, also, undertook a series of fasts, initially in an attempt to persuade the Untouchables and their leader Dr Ambedkar to reject the Government's offer to give them separate electoral representation. The very real prospect that Gandhi might die, caused Nehru immense anxiety. With his own father dead, there was almost a panic-stricken note in Nehru's enquiry in a letter to his daughter Indira, 'And whom shall I go to when I am in doubt and require wise counsel? What shall we all do when our beloved chief who inspired us and led us has gone?'

But Gandhi did not die; for one thing, the British authorities did not want the embarrassing responsibility for his death on their hands. He was released, rearrested, released once more, but he survived. Gandhi's capacity for undertaking fasts not merely perturbed Nehru but antagonized other Congress leaders such as the ambitious Subhas Bose, who rejected the Mahatma as 'an old, useless piece of furniture'.

One positive outcome of Nehru's periods in prison was the writing and publication in 1936 of his *Autobiography*. It was dedicated to his wife, who had died before its publication, and whom, as we have seen, he had come increasingly to love and respect. The book is no closely-argued political tract. Rather it reflects the self-doubt, confusion and philosophical uncertainties that characterized much of Jawaharlal's thinking. But it is, above all, an honest book, written with detachment and the capacity for self-criticism. It is the sensitive account of a man struggling to find the right path for himself and for his people.[4]

In 1936, after his return from Europe, where he had taken his wife in the hope of a last minute cure, Nehru was once more placed at the centre of affairs. During his absence he had been elected President of the Congress for 1936. This move had been masterminded by Gandhi who saw in Jawaharlal a suitable bulwark against the growth of organized socialist and communist parties within India. The left-leaning Nehru was perceived as one of the few leaders who could keep Congress reasonably united as a great, sprawling coalition of different factions and interests.

Congress also needed inspired leadership in the light of the new political situation created by the 1935 Government of India Act. This measure had been born, slowly and painfully, out of the Round Table Conferences and subsequent negotiations. Incorporating the various stages of constitutional development up to that date, the Act introduced two new and important principles: that popularly elected responsible governments should be set up in the provinces, and that the country should be organized into a federation. Federation, which would have included princely states, was in effect a dead letter from the outset. But the devolution of real and comprehensive power to the great provinces of India was a very tempting prospect for all those nationalists who had struggled so long for responsible government. Nehru was quite prepared to lead the election campaign under the new constitution, which he believed would serve to reunite Congress. The problem would arise after the election results and over the question whether Congress should co-operate with the Raj in working the new constitution. Nehru remained firmly convinced that it would be a mistake and a betrayal to take office even after an election victory.

During the protracted election campaign which lasted for eight months from 1936 into 1937, Nehru did his share of compromising, but still managed to emerge as a leader of immense popularity and stature. Covering more than 50,000 miles, he carried the message of Congress to literally millions of voters and non-voters alike. He emphasized that the fight was for Indian freedom, and that Congress would seek to combat poverty and unemployment and to improve social and cultural conditions. By the end of the campaign there was no doubt that the electorate perceived Nehru as the true and inevitable heir of Gandhi. The election results of 1937 provided Congress with an overwhelming victory. Congress had secured absolute majorities in five of the eleven provinces and was the largest single party in three others. The Muslim League did, in comparison, very badly, winning a comparatively small proportion of the Muslim vote. Nehru took the results as indicating that communalism had lost the potency of its appeal. Mohammed Ali Jinnah, leader of the Muslim League, however, drew a very different lesson: that the League should strengthen its attraction to Muslim voters by an appeal to Islamic anxieties, and also contest reserved seats in future elections in a more systematic fashion.

For the victorious Congress, the real issue was what to do with their sweeping victory. Jinnah put out feelers for a coalition but, eventually, nothing came of it. It is not too much to claim that out of this failure arose increasing antagonism between the Muslim League and Congress which was to lead along the bloody path towards partition in 1947. After three months of negotiation and close observation of the situation, Congress decided to take office under the new constitution. The main initiative for this came from the right wing of the party, and Nehru was faced with a dilemma. He solved it by not taking office himself, but trying to rally, in as constructive and progressive a fashion as possible, various Congress groupings behind the newly-formed provincial governments. The strategy here was to attempt to keep those with socialist and reforming principles allied to the party as a whole.

In the spring of 1938 Nehru found relief from the apparently intractable problems of Indian politics and took another trip to Europe. He wrote to Gandhi that the trip would 'freshen up my tired and puzzled mind'. During his time in Europe, Nehru linked his campaigning for the cause of Indian freedom with the need to confront the spread of fascism. He emphasized the British government's alleged support for the anti-republican uprising in Spain led by General Franco, and the signing of the Munich Agreement with Hitler in 1938. Thus imperialism and fascism became fused as foes to be jointly fought.

Returning to India in November 1938, Nehru faced yet another crisis. This centred on the election of the radical nationalist Subhas Bose to the presidency of Congress. At first Gandhi had promoted Bose, in the hope of being able to control him once he was installed in office. For a while Bose was contained, but by the end of 1938 his attitude became less conciliatory. Believing that war in Europe was inevitable, Bose began to argue that in that event Indian nationalism should exploit Britain's preoccupations in order to seize real freedom from the imperialist power. To the surprise and disappointment of Gandhi and the Congress right wing, Bose was elected President for 1939. Nehru attempted to mediate between the increasingly provocative Bose and his opponents within Congress. At first sight it might appear that Nehru, with his general sympathies for socialism, should have been Bose's natural ally. But Jawaharlal had already seen that, although Bose represented the quarrel within Congress as a struggle between right and left, when it came to the international scene he had proved slow to condemn the fascist regimes of Germany, Italy and Japan.

The truth was that Bose was so utterly committed to the nationalist cause, and to that of India's freedom, that he was prepared to seek the assistance of any power that would rid the sub-continent of British rule. In the final resort, Nehru was bound to side with the Gandhian centre right against the brilliant but apparently unrealistic Bose. The campaign within Congress, masterminded in many respects by Gandhi, finally succeeded in removing Bose from office in the summer of 1939. Humiliated by his own party, Bose was left to fret in the political wilderness. He eventually left India in 1941 in a doomed attempt to campaign for freedom in alliance with the Japanese.

Amid this confusion and bitterness, Nehru had to content himself with the battle to concentrate the collective mind of Congress upon the need for socialist economic planning and development. He achieved what seemed to be a triumph when the party decided to set up in 1939 a National Planning Committee with Jawaharlal as its chairman. He was ideally placed for such a position, being able to support the need for planning in such a way as to reassure those within Congress who were likely to take fright at the prospect of full-blooded socialism. He rejected class warfare, which seemed largely irrelevant to India's needs, and he was therefore generally imprecise in formulating the aims and effects of the proposed economic planning. His technique is neatly summarized in the following extract from a memorandum to the National Planning Committee of June 1939:

> The ideal of the Congress is the establishment of a free and democratic state in India. Such a free democratic state involves an egalitarian society in which equal opportunities are provided for every member for self-expression and self-fulfillment, and an adequate minimum of a civilised standard of life is assured to each member so as to make the attainment of this equal opportunity a reality. This should be the background or foundation of our Plan.[5]

In August 1939, Nehru left the problems and dilemmas of nationalist politics behind him when he left on a visit to Nationalist China as an official representative of Congress. The visit was planned to last for four weeks. But the outbreak of war in Europe at the start of September was to cut short his stay.

5

The Second World War 1939–1945

When Britain went to war with Nazi Germany on 3 September 1939, many Indian nationalists believed that full independence was almost within their grasp. The entry of Britain into the conflict, however, cruelly illustrated the sharp difference in status that still existed between India and the Dominions of the British Commonwealth. The Statute of Westminster of 1931 provided the Dominions with the constitutional right to choose whether they themselves became involved in the war. As it happened, the Dominions' reaction was predictably mixed: Australia and New Zealand considered themselves bound by the mother country's declaration of war; Canada briefly deferred her decision to the meeting of her own parliament, conscious of the need not to offend French-speaking citizens; South Africa entered the war only after a power struggle from which the pro-British Smuts faction emerged victorious, and the Irish Free State declared itself neutral. In the Indian Empire, however, the Viceroy simply announced that war had broken out between the King-Emperor and Germany. No democratic process was followed. The subordinate status of India could not have been more clearly or humiliatingly demonstrated.

Indian nationalism was faced with an exquisitely delicate dilemma. What was the war really about? Ostensibly both Britain and France had decided to fight Germany for its violation of the borders of Poland. Did the Nazi invasion of this comparatively obscure Eastern European country really necessitate the participation of the whole of the British Empire? Was not the war, in effect, really a struggle between European capitalist and imperial systems? Why should Indians, or indeed Nigerians or South Africans, sacrifice their lives to such a cause?

It was also possible, however, to see the world war in a very different light. The conflict could be interpreted as the final confrontation between expansionist fascism and western democracy, between ruthless and militaristic regimes and peace-loving parliamentary ones, between the forces of darkness and evil and the forces of light and civilization. At an emotional level, there was no doubt where the bulk of Indian nationalists and, indeed, the bulk of the Indian people stood. Obstinate, overbearing, and sometimes ruthless as the British Raj undoubtedly was, its occasional brutalities paled into insignificance beside those of Hitler's Nazi tyranny.

Nehru, returning on 9 September, discovered strong sympathy for Britain's cause. Even Gandhi, while deploring the inevitable violence of the conflict, spontaneously sided with Britain. The Muslim League, perhaps anticipating that favours would be heaped upon them, gave generally warm support to the war effort. Their hopes were to be fulfilled, and British sympathy, both open and covert, enabled the League greatly to enhance its standing and its electoral appeal during the conflict. The position of Congress was far more complicated.

Jawaharlal took an equally calculating, though different, attitude. How could India fight for the freedom of oppressed nations elsewhere if she herself was not truly free? If Britain was genuinely fighting for democracy, then surely she should hasten to eliminate imperial overlordship from India? Therefore, Nehru, and those who supported him, argued that although the Indian people would not seek to take advantage of Britain's difficulties and perils, they wanted both the freedom to participate in the war effort as they thought fit, and to have some guarantee of real independence in the very near future. Congress put pressure on the Viceroy to issue, at the very least, a declaration stating that India would be free to determine its own destiny after the war. But Lord Willingdon was in no mood to strike bargains. In his view, at least for the moment, constitutional progress should be effectively suspended. Nehru and Congress also, in effect, made an appeal that the leaders of Indian nationalism should be taken into the confidence of the Raj and associated with decisions bearing intimately on the country's involvement in the conflict.

Tragically, the Government of India was not remotely interested in these constructive proposals. Congress, failing to respond to overtures from Jinnah and the Muslim League for a common approach to the crisis, resigned from their provincial government responsibilities. The major Indian nationalist party had decided to go its own way. There was a good deal of immediate confusion. Should there be total non-cooperation, or partial non-cooperation with the authorities? For a while, Nehru, seems almost to have opted out of the dilemma. He resumed his regular spinning after a break of nearly four years, and even contemplated taking a trip to Switzerland in the summer of 1940 to see his daughter who was studying there.

The summer of 1940, however, saw the end of the 'phoney war', and the massive German offensive culminating in the fall of France and the humiliating expulsion of the British Expeditionary Force from Dunkirk. Relatively few Indian nationalists wished to exploit Britain's apparently perilous situation. Nehru for a while even opposed the proposal to restart the civil disobedience campaign, on the grounds that such a move would not be worthy of Congress. But the British authorities were in no mood to respond generously. The Viceroy seemed to represent the unyielding quality of the Raj at its worst. Equally ominous for Indian nationalism was the fact that the crisis in Europe had brought Winston Churchill to the Premiership of the United Kingdom. Churchill had spent much of his interwar years in the political wilderness denouncing what he saw as the surrender to Indian nationalist pressure. On taking office he announced that he had not become the King's first minister in order to preside over the liquidation of the British Empire.

While the Government of India demonstrated its overall determination not to compromise with Congress, it set about exploiting the mounting volume of Muslim separatist opinion. Seeing Congress as obstructionist and non-cooperative, the Raj turned to the Muslim League as a friendly faction to be used and manipulated. Favours were heaped upon the League, including funding, through the placing of lucrative government advertisements, for their newspaper *Dawn*. Jinnah and his supporters were not slow to capitalize on their increasingly favoured position. This 'playing of the Muslim card' by the British authorities was to take India one more, and lengthy, step down the path to the partition of 1947.

Gandhi, who still hoped for some sort of compromise with the Raj, requested, at the end of September 1940, an assurance from the Viceroy that there should be freedom of speech to criticize the war. If the British could meet this demand, the Mahatma assured them that there would be no need for renewed civil disobedience. To Nehru this approach smacked of desperation, even weakness, but he gave it his grudging support. In the event, Willingdon abruptly rejected Gandhi's initiative, and Congress had no option but to prepare once more for a campaign of civil disobedience. Gandhi still hoped to avoid an all-out campaign, and was content to commit the movement to non-violence and the renewed demand for freedom of speech against participation in the war. On the other hand, individuals were encouraged to carry out acts of civil disobedience.

On 30 October, Nehru became only the second Congress leader to be arrested for making a public speech against support for the war. In court he declined to plead, and instead read a lengthy statement which included the sentiments:

> It is not me that you are seeking to judge and condemn, but rather the hundreds of millions of the people of India, and that is a large task even for a proud Empire. Perhaps it may be that, though I am standing before you on my trial, it is the British Empire itself that is on its trial before the bar of the world . . . Individuals count for little . . . Seven times I have been tried and convicted by British authority in India, and many years of my life lie buried within prison walls. An eighth or ninth, and a few more years, make little difference. But it is no small matter what happens to India and her millions of sons and daughters. That is the issue before me, and that ultimately is the issue before you, Sir.[1]

Nehru received a sentence of four years' imprisonment. There was some attempt by the British authorities at home as well as in India to modify the sentence, but the Governor of the United Provinces in the end refused to back such a move. Churchill, through the Secretary of State for India, Leopold Amery, telegraphed the Viceroy in an attempt to modify the severity of the sentence. Despite this, perhaps unexpected, intervention, Nehru's imprisonment was, in comparison with earlier episodes, marked by harsh treatment.

It was almost all spent at Dehra Dun jail, to which he was no stranger. Although he was not to serve all his sentence and was released in December 1941, Nehru suffered many irksome and petty restrictions. By way of illustration, he was allowed one weekly newspaper and only six books at any particular time. He could have only one interview, and send and receive one letter every fortnight. The sending of packed meals from outside was forbidden, and he could only receive fruit if he happened to know the sender. For some time he was denied the service of a washerman or a barber, and he was obliged to buy everything he needed, such as toothpaste, through the jail staff rather than receiving it from home. Permission to attend to the business of the Congress National Planning Committee was not granted.

The intention was clearly to disrupt as far as possible his political and personal contacts with the world outside. The authorities eventually became less unbending in their treatment of Nehru, and he was no longer restricted in the number of letters that he could write each week. He had, even before this relaxation in the rules, been allowed to receive the letters written by his daughter abroad. In May 1941, Jawaharlal's personal happiness was greatly enhanced by the return of Indira and her taking up residence near Mussoorie. He could now receive visits from one of the most precious persons in his life.

From his prison cell, Nehru let it be known that Congress should not waver in its refusal to co-operate with the Raj as long as the British authorities refused to make the desired concessions in return. But these were difficult days for Congress. Not merely was the Government of India apparently unrelenting in its policy of maintaining autocratic control, but it seemed intent on encouraging and allying itself with some of the most reactionary elements in Indian society. Moreover, for the mass of the Indian people the war was not the hated affront that Congress claimed it to be. Hundreds of thousands of recruits were pouring into the British Indian Army, and the unceasing demand for war supplies for the Middle Eastern and North African fronts meant that Indian workers were receiving some of the highest wages they had ever had.

It was perhaps the apparent hopelessness of the Congress position that encouraged Subhas Bose to escape from house arrest in January 1941 and flee to Berlin, from where his broadcast voice was soon urging Indians to rise in rebellion against the hated oppressors. On 4 December 1941 the Government of India suddenly released all jailed Congressmen, including Jawaharlal. There may well have been a hidden agenda in this unexpected act of clemency. Three days later, Japanese forces attacked the United States' naval base at Pearl Harbor. Soon Japanese forces were sweeping through the Pacific, menacing the great British base at Singapore, invading Burma and threatening the frontiers of India itself. As Japan's military and naval successes mounted, an accommodation between the Raj and Congress seemed to many not merely expedient but essential. The problem was, as so often in the past, that Congress was divided as to its response. Could the Gandhian doctrine of non-violence be sustained against the imminent assault of Japanese forces? As the bombs began to fall upon Calcutta and other eastern Indian cities, *satyagraha* seemed an inadequate defence. Nehru had little faith that non-violence had any chance of repelling Japanese aggression. Many members of the Working Committee of Congress agreed, and another offer of conditional support was made to the British authorities.

In January 1942, Gandhi asked to be relieved of the leadership of Congress. The offer was accepted. Gandhi went out of his way to deny rumours of a rift between himself and Nehru:

Somebody suggested that Pandit Jawaharlal and I were estranged. It will require much more than differences of opinion to estrange us. We have had differences from the moment we became co-workers, and yet I have said for some years and say now that . . . Jawaharlal will be my successor. He says that he does not understand my language, and that he speaks a language foreign to me. This may or may not be true. But language is no bar to a union of hearts. And I know this – that when I am gone he will speak my language.[2]

During early 1942, it was difficult to see how the advance of Japanese forces on a number of fronts could be stopped. In the United States, President Roosevelt believed that India was likely to fall. In February, Winston Churchill told King George VI that in his view Burma, Ceylon, Calcutta, Madras as well as the northern part of Australia might be occupied. Nehru did not believe that in the face of a Japanese invasion, Congress and the Indian people should passively accept their fate. He argued that Congress workers should be spread out throughout the countryside organizing towns and villages to resist the enemy. India, he was determined, would not surrender without a struggle. With black-outs and air-raid precautions commonplace in those parts of India vulnerable to Japanese attack, Jawaharlal did his utmost to stem the exodus from the cities and towns and to restore people's morale. He abandoned his car for a bicycle in order to make easier and more immediate contact with the people.

On 7 March 1942, Rangoon fell to the enemy. Four days later, Churchill announced that a Labour member of the coalition Cabinet, Sir Stafford Cripps, would leave at once to attempt to achieve a reconciliation between the Raj and its Indian opponents. Cripps flew to India on a mission which was both delicate and daunting. Why did the British cabinet take this initiative? Churchill himself put it very simply when he said that the Government's desire was to 'rally all the forces of Indian life to guard their land from the menace of the invader'. With the Japanese literally at the gates of India, any attempt at reconciliation leading to a truce between the Raj and the nationalist movement would greatly strengthen Britain in its task of defending the sub-continent. It is also important to realize that the coalition Cabinet contained a substantial proportion of Labour ministers who, before the war, had been committed to the granting of full independence to India. President Roosevelt also, having signed the Atlantic Charter with Churchill undertaking to encourage the independence of people under imperial rule, put substantial pressure on Britain to give greater substance to this policy in India.

There is another, less charitable explanation. It is that Churchill resented Cripps' widespread popularity throughout the country, saw him as a potential rival, and hoped that by sending him on a mission which many thought doomed to failure he would return to the British political scene with his wings clipped. Paradoxically, if any British statesman was likely to be able to strike a deal with Congress it was Cripps. He was a high-minded, well-to-do socialist, very like Nehru. He had long been committed to the cause of Indian freedom, and his puritanical lifestyle, including his vegetarianism, was to endear him to Gandhi. Cripps also believed in his mission and in his capacity to achieve a solution.

When Cripps began his talks with Indian nationalist leaders in New Delhi on 25 March 1942, what was he offering them? The draft declaration that Cripps took with him included some offers made earlier and a number of new points. Essentially it proposed that after the war a constituent assembly, elected on a system of proportional representation by new provincial assemblies, would determine the constitution of an independent India without any interference from the British Government. Although independence would come in the form of dominion status, an independent India was conceded the right to leave the British Commonwealth if it wished. There was also an important concession to Muslim separatism in the proposal that any province would have the right to remain outside of the new Dominion. Among the other clauses was one concerning a treaty to guarantee 'British obligations'. There would be no immediate constitutional changes while the war lasted, but an interim system of government could be established composed, if it was so wished, 'of leaders of the principal sections of the Indian people'. In return for this, Britain expected the collaboration, for the duration of the war, of India's political parties.

Although the Muslim League welcomed the prospect of partition that the cabinet declaration offered, Congress was generally unhappy with this and other provisions. Among its chief concerns was the fear that dominion status might mean something less than full independence. Nor did Congress like the proposal that the princely states would be represented in any constituent assembly by their rulers rather than by representatives of the people. Gandhi opposed the declaration on the grounds of the implied partition, while the President of Congress, A. K. Azad, demanded the effective control of the nation's defence by Indian representatives.

Nehru, whom Cripps saw as crucial in the negotiations, was also anxious to ensure that the Indian people and their representatives could collaborate appropriately in the defence of the country. On the other hand, he had no time for those Congress members who argued that, as British rule was likely to be swept away by the Japanese, the movement's energies should be reserved for negotiating with the victors. Gandhi gave blunt expression to this point of view when he asked 'Why accept a post-dated cheque on a bank that is obviously failing?' Not for the first time, Nehru failed to see eye to eye with the Mahatma on this issue. Cripps, sensing that if Congress could be satisfied on the issue of national defence his mission might still succeed, secured Churchill's approval of the rewording of the paragraph on defence. He set up a meeting between Azad, Nehru and the Commander-in-Chief of the Indian Army, General Wavell.[3] Perhaps Cripps was also counting on his long-standing friendship with his fellow socialist Nehru to smooth the way to an agreement.

At all events, the initiative failed. Despite much haggling between Congress and Cripps and his advisers, their negotiations drew to a painful and sterile end. The Viceroy, backed by Churchill and Amery, firmly rejected the idea which was floated of an Indian National Government that would, in co-operation with the British authorities, run the country and be responsible for its defence. An attempt by President Roosevelt's personal representative, Colonel Johnson, to keep the talks going not merely failed, but aroused resentment on both sides. Cripps even appealed to Jawaharlal, as an old friend, to save the mission. The Congress leadership was confirmed in its suspicion that the offer lacked real substance when, in the final meeting with Cripps on 9 April 1942, they discovered that the concept of an Indian National Government had now been so eroded by various pressures that it meant virtually nothing at all.[4]

In the messy aftermath of the Cripps mission, much bitterness was expressed. Congress leaders vilified Cripps for being, in effect, the bearer of a hollow offer. Even Nehru found it 'sad beyond measure that a man like Sir Stafford Cripps should allow himself to become the Devil's Advocate'. For the Muslims, Jinnah also denounced the British proposals, arguing that they did not go far enough on the issue of self-determination, and, for good measure, attacking the briefly-discussed prospect of an independent government as a 'Fascist Grand Council and the Muslims and the other minorities . . . entirely at the mercy of Congress'.[5] Within Congress a struggle now ensued between what might be roughly described as a faction led by Gandhi and one led by Nehru. Although Jawaharlal wished for a speedy end to British rule, he did not believe that all hope of a negotiated withdrawal had ended, nor did he believe that India could be defended by any means other than by military force. For his part, Gandhi was insistent that the moment had arrived for the British to quit the sub-continent, and put his faith in *satyagraha* as a means of resisting the Japanese, and in mass civil disobedience to ameliorate conditions if Japan actually conquered India.

During the summer of 1942, Gandhi's 'Quit India' campaign began to gather massive support. Nehru and others tried to dissuade the Mahatma from his course but Gandhi was adamant and even threatened that if his 'Quit India' resolution was rejected by Congress he would leave the organization and form another. This moral blackmail carried the day, and 'Quit India' became the official policy of Congress, being confirmed at a meeting of the All-India Congress Committee in Bombay on 7 August. At the meeting of the AICC, Gandhi expressed his conviction in a semi-mystical and, to his opponents, alarming fashion:

> The voice within me tells me I shall have to fight against the whole world and stand alone! . . . Even if the whole of India tries to persuade me that I am wrong, even then I will go ahead not for India's sake alone but for the sake of the whole world. . . I cannot wait any longer for Indian freedom. I cannot wait until Mr Jinnah is converted. . . If I wait any longer, God will punish me. This is the last struggle of my life.[6]

As his arguments carried the day, Gandhi concluded 'Here is a mantra [a devotional incantation], a short one, that I give you. You may imprint it in your hearts and let every breath of yours give expression to it. The mantra is: "Do or Die". We should either free India or die in the attempt.' This could only be interpreted as a call for mass, even if non-violent, rebellion.

The Government of India responded immediately and with devastating effect. The whole of the Working Committee of Congress and a number of other party leaders were arrested. Gandhi was imprisoned in relative luxury near Poona, while Nehru and the other Congress leaders were taken to Ahmadnagar Fort. This was Nehru's ninth imprisonment, and his longest, since he was not released until June 1945, when the war in Europe was over.

The arrest of the Congress leadership provoked a huge and immediate response from millions of Indian people. Demonstrations, strikes and acts of civil disobedience were widespread. The Government of India panicked and increased its repression. Congress was declared an illegal organization and its assets and records confiscated; curfews were imposed and assemblies of more than five people banned; there were mass arrests and, predictably, violent and tragic confrontations. Although the Raj eventually restored order, grave consequences flowed from the arrest of the Congress leaders. Into the vacuum that had been created, flooded a tide of revolutionaries and troublemakers. Activists of right and left took the chance of asserting their views and often encouraging acts of sabotage and violence. Large sections of the railway system were effectively put out of operation for a while, government buildings were set ablaze and a number of so-called collaborators killed. The British response was implacable: troops fired on crowds, aircraft bombed and machine-gunned demonstrators, and in some places public executions were staged.

By the end of the year the uprising was virtually finished. The Indian Army had stayed loyal, and many elements in the country had kept their distance from the rebellion. The failure of the 'Quit India' movement not merely gave comfort to the British Government, who were able to denounce Congress as unrepresentative of the people as a whole, but allowed both the Muslim League and the exiled Subhas Bose to present their alternative agendas more powerfully. This had two effects. One was that when the British authorities were obliged, as they inevitably were, to reopen negotiations about India's future independence, the Muslim League had made so much progress among India's Islamic community that it could claim almost equal standing with Congress. The other was that Bose was able to mount a military challenge to the Raj's authority. The challenge was admittedly an ineffectual one, but at the outset this was not clear. Bose had been allowed by the Japanese to appeal to Indian officers and men who had been taken prisoners of war to join the newly formed Indian National Army. Some 20,000 men responded to the invitation to wage war against the Raj at the side of Japanese forces. The threat posed was more prospective than real, and Bose's death in an aircraft accident as the war was ending brought the unhappy episode to its conclusion.

How meanwhile did Nehru make use of his longest term in prison, the one thousand and forty days from 9 August 1942 to 15 June 1945? He did a great deal to keep up morale amongst the Congress detainees by organizing and supervising a regular community life. Duties were allotted to each person, and Jawaharlal himself took apparently great pleasure in the gardening activities that were allowed. Between April and September 1944 he also wrote another book, *The Discovery of India*. It is long, at times rambling and repetitive, and partly autobiographical. It contains a lengthy survey of India's culture before the arrival of the British. It also shows a clear moving away from a purely Marxist analysis of social and political problems. Primarily, of course, the book was meant to send an optimistic and stirring message to the Indian people: that many of the nation's problems had been accentuated by alien rule, and that once free of British control much that was wrong in Indian society could be put to rights.[7]

By the end of 1944, as the Allied Armies swept into Germany itself, and as the Red Army continued its drive from the east, it was evident that the fighting in Europe would soon be over. Quite apart from the rebellion that had accompanied the 'Quit India' campaign, the war had had a profound economic and social effect upon millions of Indian subjects. Nearly two million recruits had been taken into the Army, the demand for labour had brought men out of the villages into the cities, and even women had found employment in offices and in the Women's Army Corp that had previously been denied them. Countless Indians, therefore, felt a greater sense of self-respect and achievement. But there was also dangerous inflation, and a rapid rise in food prices.

In these circumstances the new Viceroy, Lord Wavell, during his visit to the United Kingdom in March 1945, pressed the British coalition Government to make meaningful and urgent concessions to Indian nationalism. The Cabinet agreed, but before anything could be done Germany had surrendered and the coalition Government had resigned. There was to be a general election, and in the meantime a 'caretaker' Government of Conservatives was formed, headed by Churchill. With Churchill's blessing the Viceroy left for India with a brief to begin serious negotiations with the nationalists.

On 14 June 1945, Wavell returned to India and made public the new proposals. These did not fundamentally differ from those offered in 1942, although the Viceroy's executive council would now consist entirely of Indians, save for the Viceroy himself and the Commander-in-Chief. The Muslim League was further encouraged by the offer of equal representation for Hindus and Muslims on this council. This concession was not merely a recognition of Muslim support during the war, but an acknowledgement that there were now effectively two nations in India, as Jinnah had for so long argued. The Viceroy invited an assortment of political leaders to meet him at a conference to discuss the proposals on 25 June in the hill-station of Simla. Nehru and other Congress leaders were released from prison to facilitate the negotiations. But the conference brought little joy to Congress who were affronted by Wavell's unabashed support for Jinnah and the Muslim League. The discussions ended on 14 July, with Jinnah in such a powerful position that he could effectively veto any further constitutional proposals of which he disapproved.

After the conference Nehru went to Kashmir for a holiday. While he was there a Labour Government was swept to overwhelming power in Britain at the general election. Churchill, long regarded as the unremitting opponent of Indian nationalism, was defeated and replaced by Attlee, who was committed to the principle of independence for India. The new administration, as the war against Japan ended with the dropping of two atomic bombs, made its position clear on 15 August 1945. The King's speech from the throne contained the words 'my Government will do their utmost to promote, in conjunction with the leaders of Indian opinion, the early realisation of full self-government in India'. The stage was now set for the drama of the final negotiations for India's independence.

6
The Last, Slow Steps to Freedom 1945–1947

To many Indian nationalists, the new Labour Government in Britain proved, at least initially, to be a grievous disappointment. As the historian R. J. Moore puts it, 'Labour entered office keen to fulfil the promise of early self-government for India. Their imperialist inheritance was an impediment.'[1] Far from flinging open the gates of freedom, the Attlee administration took some time to marshal its thoughts on the Indian problem and to take the appropriate steps to bring it to a satisfactory resolution. Despite the anti-imperialistic rhetoric and the genuine encouragement of colonial freedom movements by Labour politicians and activists during the inter-war years, once in power the Attlee Cabinet were determined to behave responsibly on the issue of Empire.

This cautious approach to the encouragement and implementation of colonial freedom at least partly reflected the conservative views of a number of leading ministers; chief among these were Ernest Bevin and Herbert Morrison. Nor was the Prime Minister, taciturn, inscrutable and pipe-smoking, a revolutionary bent on the prompt dissolution of the British Empire. Nehru had earlier made personal contact with leading members of the Labour party at Filkins, Sir Stafford Cripps's country house, during his visit of June 1938. Among the house guests were Clement Attlee, Aneurin Bevan, and members of Labour's Shadow Cabinet, as well as the influential Harold Laski, a Professor at the London School of Economics and a member of the National Executive Committee. The Labour Government's failure to find an early solution to the problem of Indian independence was a source of irritation and disappointment to Nehru. He may well have agreed with the Viceroy, Wavell, who wryly observed in December 1946: 'Bevan like everyone else hates the idea of our leaving India, but like everyone else has no alternative to suggest.'[2]

Of course, there were pressures pushing the other way. They meant that, in the last resort, the Labour administration of 1945-51 would be associated with the first great act of decolonization, not to speak of the abandonment of the Palestine Mandate and the final establishment of an independent Irish Republic. The mass of the voters who had put Labour into power did not necessarily want, when they thought about it at all, an indefinite extension of Imperial rule. What they did want was the rapid demobilization of the armed forces, together with full employment and the establishment of the welfare state at home. In the case of India, not merely was full independence desirable and apparently within easy reach, but the cost, both moral and material, of a protracted British attempt to hold on to power by force was unthinkable.

For the last few months of 1945, the Government in effect marked time, perhaps prudently waiting to see the outcome of the central and provincial Indian elections fixed for the end of the year. The last elections for the central assembly had been held in 1934 and for the provincial legislatures in 1937. The elections would provide, among other things, a crucial indication of the electoral strength of the Muslim League. Jinnah and his supporters went all out for a result that would establish beyond all reasonable doubt the necessity of creating a Muslim homeland, to be called Pakistan. The spectre of a united India dominated by an unsympathetic Hindu majority was vividly and unscrupulously conjured up by League candidates. For their part, Congress made its usual broad appeal to a wide spectrum of interests. They hoped to disguise the divisions within the party on the issue of the possible establishment of Pakistan by claiming that the real purpose of the election was to enable the voters to show their overwhelming support for Indian freedom.

A surprisingly low-key election campaign was given an unexpected shot in the arm by the Government of India's determination to put on trial and suitably punish those who had taken up arms in Bose's Indian National Army. Although Nehru and most Congress leaders had, at best, ambivalent attitudes towards the INA, they saw in the Government's apparent vindictiveness a chance to raise the issue to their electoral advantage. As early as August 1945, Nehru had argued that the soldiers of the INA should not be treated as ordinary rebels, and that to punish them 'would in effect be a punishment on all India and all Indians, and a deep wound would be created in millions of hearts'. The Government indicated that they would be prepared to deal leniently with the rank and file, but insisted that the leaders and those accused of atrocities must be brought to trial. By the middle of September 1945 the All India Congress Committee came out in defence of the accused officers, arguing that they were only guilty of 'having laboured, however mistakenly, for the freedom of India'. A Defence Committee was set up by Congress to help those accused.

The British authorities pushed ahead, however, with a show trial which was staged in November 1945 in the Red Fort at Delhi. Three former Indian Army officers who had held high rank in the INA were charged with, in effect, treason. With either exquisite sensibility or extreme tactlessness, of the three officers accused one was a Hindu, one a Muslim and the third a Sikh. India's three major religious communities were thus all likely to be equally antagonized by the trial. As public interest in the trial intensified, seventeen lawyers appeared for the defence. Nehru was one of these, putting on his barrister's gown once more after a lapse of over twenty-five years. Despite a spirited and complex defence, the accused men were found guilty and sentenced to be cashiered and transported for life to penal settlements. There was an immediate outcry and the British authorities backed down, remitting the sentences of transportation although confirming the other penalties. It was also announced that there would be no more trials of returning INA soldiers, except those accused of atrocities.

Congress, through its resolute defence of the accused, had won a significant propaganda victory. It had also revitalized its electoral appeal, an appeal that was enhanced as the three, effectively acquitted, accused officers toured the country to a rapturous mass reception. Unfortunately for those who still hoped for a free and united India, Congress's renewed appeal to the electorate only succeeded in pushing Jinnah and the League into making the issue of partition and the establishment of Pakistan central to the election. Muslim separatism was further provoked by the impression given by some Congress leaders that, once the British had gone, they would resolve the communal conflict themselves, by 'civil war if necessary'.

The result of the election confirmed the remarkable progress of the Muslim League. In the central assembly the League won all the reserved Muslim seats with 86.6 per cent of the vote. In the provinces where Muslims formed the majority of the population, however, the League did not win a majority of votes. Its vote in the Punjab, for instance, was 46.56 per cent and in Sind 45.75 per cent, while in the North West Frontier Province it only succeeded in achieving 37.19 per cent. But in terms of seats gained, the League did spectacularly, perhaps unfairly, well. Nonetheless Congress was able to form ministries in eight of the eleven provinces, and the League only in Bengal and Sind, with the Punjab ruled by a coalition Unionist Party supported by Congress. Despite the different ways of interpreting the election results, Jinnah's assertion that the Muslim League was the true, indeed the only, voice of Islam in India seemed to have firm foundations. With the battle lines being drawn up between Congress and the League, the Labour government responded somewhat indecisively with the sending of a parliamentary delegation to reassure Indians of the Cabinet's sincerity of purpose. Perhaps the Government's intention was to gain an up-to-date impression of the situation from the returning delegation.

At all events, the Government was shaken out of its apparent lethargy by the mutinies of early 1946. The first of these, in the middle of January, was all the more shocking as it took place among British RAF servicemen infuriated by delays over demobilization and repatriation. Although the men were easily placated, units of the Indian Air Force were the next to mutiny. Much worse was to follow. In February a naval mutiny broke out at Bombay. The Bombay mutiny was followed by others at Calcutta, at Madras, and at Karachi where the local Army commander actually opened fire on rebel ships causing considerable casualties. Although the mutinies were quite soon quelled, they had the effect of galvanizing the Government into activity. Clement Attlee announced that a delegation of senior cabinet ministers would leave directly for India to meet political leaders and to search for a solution to the problems of India's constitutional future. The Cabinet Mission consisted of the Secretary of State for India, Lord Pethick-Lawrence (soon derided by his critics as 'Pathetic Lawrence'), Sir Stafford Cripps, and A. V. Alexander, First Lord of the Admiralty. Of these, Cripps was clearly the key figure.

It was made plain that the basis of the negotiations with the Cabinet Mission should be the independence of India. The mission would set up appropriate consultative machinery to decide upon the form of the independence constitution. It would be entirely for Indians to decide upon their future form of government. Eventually a Constituent Assembly, composed of delegates elected by the provincial assemblies, would draft an all-India constitution. If any province chose to opt out of the proceedings, it would simply be bypassed until it wished to re-enter the negotiations. Whether the state of Pakistan should be established or not should be settled, either by the agreement of the leading political parties, or through a plebiscite of all the inhabitants of the areas concerned. An independent India would also be free to leave the Commonwealth if it so wished.

Soon after arriving in India, the Cabinet Mission realized that the apparently liberal policy of leaving things to Indians to settle for themselves would only bring the negotiations back to the main stumbling block, whether or not a Muslim state should be established. With neither Congress nor the League able to agree, the Cabinet Mission put forward its own proposals. These consisted of the establishment of a union government which would deal with foreign affairs, defence and communications; two groups of provinces, one predominantly Hindu and the other predominantly Muslim, dealing with matters of common interest; all residuary powers should be invested in the provinces.

A conference met at Simla to consider whether these proposals formed the basis of a settlement. At the conference, it first appeared that Jinnah was not pressing for the establishment of a sovereign state. For his part, Nehru stated that Congress would not compel any Muslim-dominated province to stay in an all-India federation. As a result of this apparent accord, the Cabinet Mission drew up on 8 May 'Suggested Points for Agreement'. While proposing an all-India government and legislature, composed of equal proportions from the Muslim-majority and Hindu-majority provinces, and dealing with matters like foreign affairs, defence, and communications, the suggestions included the phrase 'Groups of provinces may be formed'. All parties, including the Viceroy, recognized the phrase 'may be formed' as a vital concession to Congress, since the word 'may' seemed to keep open the door for a united India. But although Congress insisted that any groupings should be optional, Jinnah and the League were not convinced. Amicable discussions between Nehru and Jinnah could not resolve the impasse. Soon Jinnah was asserting that the question of partition had already been settled by the Muslim vote at the recent elections, but conceded that he was prepared for the sovereignty of Pakistan to be delegated within a loose and limited union, provided that sovereignty was recognized in the form of a group of provinces. Nehru responded that a strong central government was required, and that essentially Congress did not agree with the League on the issue of partition.

Despairing of further progress, the Cabinet Mission decided to issue its own plan. These proposals clearly rejected the idea of partition. There would be an Indian union, dealing with foreign affairs, defence and communications, with the necessary authority to raise appropriate finance. Any major communal issue brought to the central legislature would require a majority of each community as well as an overall majority before it became law. All other powers would be vested in the provinces, which would be enabled to form groups with a great deal of autonomy. The arrangement of the union and the groupings could be reconsidered every ten years. There were also clear plans for the election of the Constituent Assembly which would determine the final constitutional settlement. The Mission also advocated the immediate formation of an interim government. What the Mission was offering was a mechanism for ending deadlock and enabling India to obtain independence 'in the shortest time and with the least danger of internal disturbance and conflict'.³ Both Congress and the League proceeded to interpret the plan, particularly the reference to groups, to their own advantage.

Nehru was depressed by the failure to arrive at a speedy and mutually acceptable solution. He also turned his attention to the problem of the princely states. How were these provinces, some huge and some minute, to be peacefully incorporated into the proposed union of India? Would their frequently autocratic rulers, for so long sustained by the British, willingly set aside their power and allow democracy to flourish? In June 1946, Nehru was actually arrested for illegally crossing the frontier of Kashmir where the Maharajah had arrested Sheikh Abdullah and other leaders of the National Conference who were either members or supporters of Congress. Although he was soon released, the incident was a demonstration of the continuing power of the Indian princes.

At the end of June 1946 the Cabinet Mission departed, leaving it to Lord Wavell to negotiate the formation of the interim government that was a central part of the Mission's plan. It was only possible to proceed on the assumption that both Congress and the League had agreed to the process. Nehru, however, created confusion by asserting the Congress line, 'We are not bound by a single thing except that we have decided to go into the Constituent Assembly.'⁴ Jinnah now swooped on Nehru's remarks and used them as a justification for withdrawing the League's apparent acceptance of the plan.

As President of the Congress, Nehru was now asked by the Viceroy to submit proposals for the formation of an interim government and, if possible, to get Jinnah to agree to the plans before they were laid on the table. Predictably the Nehru–Jinnah talks failed. For a while it seemed that the British authorities would work with Congress to the detriment of the League, but Wavell would have none of this and sought once more to appease the Muslims.

Doubtless he felt justified in making this move by the terrible consequences of the Muslim League's Direct Action Day, called for 16 August 1946. The main trouble-spot was Calcutta where the Muslim League Prime Minister of Bengal, Hussein Shaheed Suhrawardy, displayed a shamefully partisan attitude as the communal killings escalated out of control. By 21 August unofficial estimates put the number of dead, both Hindu and Muslim, at over fifteen thousand. Communal rioting spread to other areas.

Against this grim background, Nehru firmly insisted that the proposed ministry should be a strong and stable government even if the League was unwilling to join it. The ministry Nehru wanted consisted of fifteen members, five 'caste Hindus', five Muslims, one scheduled caste and four minority representatives. He got his way, and the Viceroy announced the list of ministers. Nehru was vice-president of the executive council of this interim government, holding the portfolios of external affairs and Commonwealth relations.

But the interim government would lack substance if still boycotted by the League. Urgent attempts were made to bring the Muslim League into the interim administration. Jinnah, who had no desire to be left out of office, was eventually persuaded, after negotiations with Nehru and the granting of some concessions by Congress, that it would be possible to join the government. As it happened, the Congress–League accord were disrupted by Wavell who brought Jinnah and his nominees unconditionally into the government. Reluctantly Congress accepted this. The interim government was a demonstrable failure. Congress and the League acted as rival factions, and in any case the executive had little real power.

Meanwhile it was inevitably proving complicated, if not downright impossible, to set up the Constituent Assembly with the agreement of all parties. But after more concessions were made to the League this constitutional body met on 9 December 1946. Its work was piecemeal and frequently disrupted, particularly by the League. In effect, Jinnah could, by threatening to withdraw, destroy the whole process. By the end of January 1947 obstruction by the League and by the Indian princes had effectively destroyed the Assembly's work. As communal rioting spread across northern India, the nine non-Muslim League members of the government informed the Viceroy that in their opinion the League could not continue in the administration. Nehru and his colleagues threatened resignation. The Viceroy put pressure on Congress for further concessions. Jinnah seemed to be still dictating the course of events.

The British Government, however, now acted decisively to break the deadlock and to hurry events along. On 20 February 1947, the Prime Minister announced in the House of Commons that the British would withdraw from India no later than June 1948. This meant that there would be a transfer of power into responsible Indian hands by that date, but in February 1947 it was not at all clear whose those hands might be. Addressing this problem, Attlee's statement contained, in effect, an ultimatum:

> His Majesty's Government will have to consider to whom the powers of the Central Government of British India should be handed over, on the due date, whether to some form of Central Government for British India or in some

areas to the existing Provincial Governments, or in such a way as may be most reasonable and in the best interests of the Indian people.

Further, the Prime Minister, recognizing Wavell's reputation for pro-Muslim partiality, and growing impatient with his defeatist attitude, announced that there would be a new Viceroy. The replacement would be Earl Mountbatten of Burma. This appointment signalled in the most dramatic way the Government's determination to breakout from the constitutional and communal wranglings of the past and to make a fresh start in India.

7
Partition and Freedom 1947–1948

Lord Mountbatten was sworn in as Viceroy on 24 March 1947. He had less than five months to accomplish a transfer of power of a complexity and significance hitherto unknown in British imperial history. This, the last and briefest viceroyalty, was also to be one of the most decisive and momentous. Mountbatten came to his task with unique and indeed unrivalled qualifications. Royal blood flowed in his veins, and it was entirely appropriate that the last Viceroy should also be a great-grandson of Queen Victoria and a cousin of the last King-Emperor George VI. After a distinguished record of active service in the Royal Navy, Mountbatten had finally been appointed Supreme Allied Commander in South East Asia. He had, therefore, an intimate knowledge of Indian forces, the sub-continent and the surrounding area. It is significant that, when created an Earl, he took the title of Mountbatten of Burma. As if these qualifications were insufficient, Mountbatten and his intelligent and vivacious wife, Edwina, were known to be Labour sympathizers and in general supporters of the cause of colonial freedom.

Nehru and Mountbatten already knew each other relatively well. In March 1946, during Nehru's trip to Malaya, Mountbatten had arranged for Jawaharlal to be received at the airport in Singapore with all the ceremonial courtesy owed to a man destined to be India's future Prime Minister. The two men had also come to a compromise over Nehru's desire to pay a visit to a small memorial built to the Indian National Army by some of its personnel. The memorial was an affront to the British authorities who had frequently caused it to be pulled down, only to see it rebuilt by INA sympathizers. In response to Mountbatten's wishes, Nehru avoided a public function at the memorial, but compromised by visiting it quietly, almost as a private individual.

The two men had much in common. They had been born to privilege and power, were used to exercising authority and were both inclined to shows of personal vanity. There is also some evidence that Nehru saw in Mountbatten another authoritative personality to whom he could become attached, not exactly a father-figure, but certainly one representing power and prestige. At any rate, there could be no doubting the close personal and working relationship that soon developed between the two men.

Nor was this all. It seems clear that a passionate friendship developed between Nehru and Lady Mountbatten. The Mountbattens' marriage had been marked previously by various acts of infidelity on both sides, perhaps more on her part than his. Although historians have haggled over the details, the intimate relationship that developed between Nehru and Lady Mountbatten seems not to have disrupted Jawaharlal's friendship with the Viceroy and, arguably, to have enhanced it. Lord Mountbatten's official biographer writes of a relationship that was 'intensely loving, romantic, trusting, generous, idealistic, even spiritual', although he adds, rather curiously, 'If there was any physical element it can only have been of minor importance to either party'. Mountbatten was later to write to his wife 'I am very glad that you realise that I know and have always understood the very special relationship between Jawaharlal and you, made easier by my fondness and admiration for him, and by the remarkably lucky fact that among my many defects God did not add jealousy in any shape or form.'[1] The formation of this remarkable triangular relationship certainly does not seem to have affected the transfer of power for the worse.

For the first six weeks of Mountbatten's viceroyalty, Nehru was not at the forefront of negotiations. Much of his energies were devoted to the Asian Relations Conference that met in New Delhi from 23 March to 2 April 1947. The conference was chiefly the product of Nehru's commitment to internationalism. It was an attempt to give non-official expression to all shades of opinion in the countries of Asia, including Egypt. Thus the views of both the Chinese Communists and the Kuomintang, and of the Arab League as well as delegates from Palestine's Hebrew University were expressed. The Soviet Union, Britain, the United States and a few other western powers sent observers.

The conference met in an atmosphere of optimism and purpose, as if the delegates were conscious that the post-war world offered them all unprecedented opportunities for development and co-operation. Although there was no second session of the Asian Relations Conference, the precedent set was significant. The fact that it had taken place, and in such a positive fashion, almost certainly had a substantial influence on the later decision to hold the Asian–African Conference at Bandung in 1955, an event which provided a watershed in the developing relations between the western powers and what came to be known as the Third World.

While Nehru was preoccupied with the Asian Relations Conference, the Viceroy and his advisers produced a 'Plan Balkan'. In essence, this plan initially devolved power to the provinces, including the princely states, who would then be left to decide whether they would form into any groups, allowing them to negotiate deals with central government before being integrated into what was effectively a weak union. The chaos that could have ensued if such a plan had been implemented can only be imagined. With power at the centre so uncertain, conceivably any number of new states could emerge from the confusion. Quite apart from Pakistan, which the now dying Jinnah and the League were bent on creating at almost any cost, there could have been an independent Hyderabad or Kashmir, and it has been argued that there 'could have been an independent Bengal, and there certainly would have been two Punjabs'.[2] Such a 'Balkanization' would have been a sad, inept and paradoxical conclusion to nearly two centuries of British centralizing rule.

Mountbatten had originally intended to unveil these proposals at a meeting with Indian Nationalist leaders on 17 May. On 8 May the Viceroy invited Nehru, his daughter, Indira, and Krishna Menon, to join him and Lady Mountbatten as personal guests at the Viceregal Lodge at Simla. On the evening of the 10 May, Mountbatten, alone in his study with Nehru after dinner, decided, on a 'hunch' as he later described it, to show his guest a copy of the secret plan. It was an act of good faith, doubtless, and an indication not only of Mountbatten's liking for Nehru but also of his alleged partiality for Congress as opposed to the League. The Viceroy explained his motives frankly the next day: 'Last night, having made real friends with Nehru during his stay here, I asked him whether he would look at the London draft, as an act of friendship and on the understanding that he would not utilise his prior knowledge or mention to his colleagues that he had seen it.'[3]

Nehru did not even begin to read the file that he had been given until he had returned to his bedroom. Its contents horrified him and reduced him to rage and disappointment. The next day he wrote in a 'Personal and Secret' letter to Mountbatten that the proposals had 'produced a devastating effect upon me ... The whole approach was completely different from what ours had been and the picture of India that emerged frightened me ... a picture of fragmentation and conflict and disorder, and, unhappily also, of a worsening of relations between India and Britain.'[4] Dismayed by Nehru's furious reaction, although probably relieved that he had at least shown him the plan prior to the meeting of 17 May, Mountbatten hastened to mend broken fences. The 17 May meeting was postponed and he instructed his advisers to refashion the proposals in a way that would meet Nehru's and Congress's objections.

The plan that subsequently emerged was acceptable to Congress because it reasserted the concept of an Indian state as a continuing entity, while allowing for the secession of those provinces where the majority of the inhabitants desired such a move. Nor would the plan apply to the princely states. The Constituent Assembly would continue to meet, and there would also be a second Constituent Assembly for those areas which chose not to join in the work of the existing assembly. Arrangements were provided for the partitioning, and the subsequent boundary demarcations of states like Bengal and the Punjab. The continuing problem of the North–West Frontier Province was to be solved by making a concession to the League. If, as expected, the Punjab decided on partition, a referendum would be held in the NWFP under the authority of the Governor-General and in collaboration with the provincial government.

While nationalist leaders were digesting and generally approving these proposals, the horrifying spread of communal violence in places like Lahore and Calcutta caused Nehru and his colleagues to demand an immediate transfer of power in order to bring about a restoration of order. Mountbatten, while indicating his sympathy with Nehru's impatience, induced him to agree to the proposed referendum in the NWFP and also to accept dominion status. Both the British Government and the Viceroy had from the outset wanted an independent India, whether partitioned or not, to remain within the Commonwealth. Despite some protests from within Congress, the principle of dominion status was accepted as a means of speeding the transfer of power. In any event, dominion status could easily be ditched in future, as the Irish Free State was very soon to demonstrate.

By early June 1947 the British and all the major parties concerned had agreed upon the process to be followed. On the evening of 3 June, Mountbatten broadcast to the nation, outlining the agreement. He was followed by Nehru, Jinnah and Baldev Singh, the representative of the Sikhs. Nehru's speech included an assessment of the last nine months when Congress had been in office at the centre of affairs, weighing the achievements against the tragedies and failures, and offering a sober acceptance of the principle of secession.

> We are little men serving a great cause, but because the cause is great something of that greatness falls upon us also. Mighty forces are at work in

the world today and in India, and I have no doubt that we are ushering in a period of greatness for India. The India of geography, of history and tradition, the India of our minds and hearts, cannot change.[5]

The process of implementing the plan now went ahead. The date for the transfer of power had been set at 15 August 1947. With the establishment of an independent Pakistan now inevitable, a Partition Committee was set up, chaired by the Viceroy and with a number of representative Indian members. Beneath this committee was a structure of sub-committees and expert committees which would deal with a whole range of topics from the fixing of boundaries to the division of the armed forces.

The partitioning of Bengal and Punjab was more or less a formality, but one of the chief problems lay in the future of the NWFP. In the event, the proposed referendum produced an extremely narrow majority of the electorate in favour of joining Pakistan, against a background of the abstention of Congress supporters in the province. Despite the enormous scale of the task, the process of opinion-taking, voting, and arranging partition proceeded relatively smoothly.

The future of the princely states, however, seemed to pose a particularly complex problem. As British agents and political departments were withdrawn from these provinces, some of them openly prepared for independence, expanding their armies and acquiring modern weapons. Despite the pretensions of some of their rulers, before 15 August, all the princely states save three had acceded to one or other of the two new Dominions. These three were Kashmir, Hyderabad and Junagadh. Nehru's interest in Kashmir was of an intimate and long-standing nature. Hyderabad was a very large state at the centre of the country, which had even in the recent past sought territorial access to the sea in order to advance its economic future. In contrast, Junagadh was a comparatively small state of some 4,000 square miles on the coast north of Bombay. The problem of these three non-acceding provinces, however, would have to wait for a solution until after the transfer of power.

At midnight on 14 August the British Raj came to an end. As two new nations were born, Nehru made one of his most moving speeches.

> Long years ago we made a tryst with destiny, and now the time comes when we shall redeem our pledge, not wholly or in full measure, but very substantially. At the stroke of the midnight hour, when the world sleeps, India will awake to life and freedom. A moment comes, which comes but rarely in history, when we step out from the old to the new, when an age ends, and when the soul of a nation long suppressed finds utterance.[6]

The pomp and ceremony that attended the transfer of power, and the unaffected joy with which it was greeted, merely masked a unfolding tragedy of enormous dimensions. As millions of people migrated to one or other of the two new Dominions, the communal violence and killings which had been a prelude to independence grew in ferocity and scale. There are varying computations as to how many Indians lost their lives during the mass migrations, but a figure of half a million seems a reasonable estimate. Both Nehru and Gandhi did their utmost to put an end to the violence and to protect the rights of minorities. As the new Prime Minister of independent India, Nehru's voice carried great weight, but the crisis made him once more draw closer to Gandhi as the man who had founded his political career upon the principle of non-violence. The assistance of Mountbatten, as Governor-General, was also requested by Nehru.

During the last months of 1947, Nehru paid almost daily visits to Gandhi, apparently gaining much spiritual and psychological sustenance as a result. The Mahatma himself was greatly agitated by the hideous spectacle of communal violence, and concerned by rumours that Congress politicians were already taking bribes from businessmen and others, profiting from the black market and the like. As a result, Gandhi resorted once more to the weapon of fasting.

The hatred which Gandhi's peacemaking activities aroused amongst many fanatical Hindus led to plots to assassinate him. An attempt to blow him up with a bomb at a prayer meeting on 20 January 1948 failed. During the subsequent interrogations, the police learnt of a continuing plot to assassinate the Mahatma, but inexplicably, and perhaps suspiciously, did very little to follow up their clues. On 30 January Gandhi was shot at point-blank range by a young man dressed in khaki who had attracted his attention by calling out 'Bapuji, Bapuji' ('Father, Father'). The Mahatma gasped 'Oh, God', and collapsed, to die almost immediately. Mountbatten, when informed of the tragedy amid calls for revenge upon the suspected Muslim assassin, cried out with great presence of mind, 'You fool! Don't you know it was a Hindu?' Although Mountbatten did not know at that moment that the assassin was indeed a Hindu, his quick reaction had the effect of avoiding what could have been another terrible chapter of communal violence and massacre.

The personal blow of Gandhi's death to Nehru was overwhelming. He rushed to the scene of the assassination where he 'bent his head down and began to sob like a child'. A few hours later, urged by Mountbatten to broadcast to the nation, Nehru gave a deeply moving and appropriate expression to his grief and to the loss which the death of Gandhi implied:

Friends and comrades, the light has gone out of our lives and there is darkness everywhere. . . . The light has gone out, I said, and yet I was wrong. For the light that shone in this country was no ordinary light . . . That light represented something more that the immediate present, it represented the living, the eternal truths, reminding us of the right path, drawing us from error, taking this ancient country to freedom. . . A great disaster is a symbol to us to remember all the good things of life and forget the small things of which we have thought too much. In his death he has reminded us of the big things of life, the living truth, and if we remember that, then it will be well with India.[6]

There can be no doubting the intense and profound grief that Nehru felt at the death of the man whom he had come to regard as a second father. He was also sorely to miss the spiritual and emotional support that he had received from his friend. But Gandhi's removal from the political scene was not without its political advantages. A sometimes complicating, always powerful influence had gone. From now onwards, Nehru was to be entirely his own master.

8

Prime Minister 1948–1956

The first few years of India's independence, from 1947 to 1951, were years of transition. Although he was Prime Minister, Nehru's position within the Cabinet was complicated at least until the end of 1950 by his rivalry with his colleague Vallabhbhai Patel. If anyone could challenge Nehru for the leadership of the new India, it was Patel. He was a Congress party boss from Gujarat, who was identified with political authoritarianism, Hindu orthodoxy and the interests of big business. He had been, with Nehru, one of the leading members of the Interim Government of 1946–7. Subsequently, until his death in 1950, he held the powerful positions of Deputy Prime Minister and Minister for Home Affairs, the States, Information and Broadcasting. If Patel drew most of his support from the right wing of Congress, Nehru was still associated with the left. Jawaharlal, despite the vicissitudes, disappointments and failures that were to come, stood for idealism, socialism (albeit in an Indian form), and internationalism.

Patel's ability to mount a serious challenge to Nehru's premiership had been fatally undermined, however, by Gandhi's assassination. Tarred, however unfairly, with the brush of Hindu, right-wing, fundamentalism, Patel would now have been inadequately trusted by too much of the Congress movement to make a bid for the Prime Minister's office. Instead he busied himself with the onerous work that his portfolios imposed upon him, showing particular finesse and political determination in carrying through the integration of the various provinces into the new India.

But Patel died in December 1950, and Nehru was able to make, in Parliament, a graceful speech of appreciation for a dead colleague and veteran of the independent struggle. In truth, he must have been glad to be rid of him, for among their many differences, had been Patel's early attempt to diminish the role of Prime Minister. Patel had wanted the Premier's functions reduced to those of a benevolent umpire, ensuring that there was no conflict between the ministries, and leaving ministers to get on with the job of implementing policy and the decisions of the Cabinet. Although Patel's views on this matter did not prevail, the policy differences between himself and Nehru did not cease, and some unseemly disputes ensued. Before his death, Patel, almost as a last throw, managed to get a candidate representing the right wing of Congress confirmed as President for 1950. This nominee, P. D. Tandon, was to give Nehru considerable trouble through to the autumn of 1951 when, after much conflict between them and the Prime Minister's threat to resign, Tandon himself resigned his position. From that time onwards, the supremacy of Nehru was never seriously challenged. He could now invite those who had left the party to rejoin, and make a powerful appeal for unity and the rejection of communal rivalries. Speaking in October 1951, Nehru declared: 'If any person raises his hand to strike down another on the ground of religion, I shall fight him to the last breath of my life, both as the head of the government and from outside.'[1]

One of the major problems to be resolved after independence was the future of the three princely states that had not yet acceded to either India or Pakistan. All three, Junagadh, Hyderabad, and Kashmir, offered potential conflict between Muslim and Hindu interests, and between the two new Dominions. In Junagadh, the difficulty was that a predominantly Hindu population was ruled by a Muslim Nawab. The Nawab had opted for Pakistan, but the state was several hundred miles away from West Pakistan and there was no real prospect of joining the new country. After a few weeks of diplomacy, Indian troops simply occupied Junagadh and an ensuing plebiscite resulted in a decisive vote for union with India. Although Pakistan protested at this action there was little that the government at Karachi could do about it.

Hyderabad, however, was in a different category. Again, it had a large Hindu majority, some 85 per cent of the population, but it had also a tradition of Muslim government going back to Mogul times. The province was, however, completely surrounded by Indian territory and to have allowed its continued existence as an independent, and even potentially hostile, state made little geographical or political sense. For some months the ruler, the Nizam, played for time and made various appeals to Pakistan, to Lord Mountbatten as Governor General, and even to Portugal, with whom a secret treaty was signed granting Hyderabad the use of the harbour facilities of the colony of Goa. Nehru wished to avoid military intervention, but by September 1948 even he could resist this solution no longer, and a contingent of the Indian Army was sent into the province, allegedly in a 'police action', to restore law and order. Hyderabad was incorporated into the Indian union with a minimum of fuss.

Kashmir presented problems of a completely different kind. Geographically adjacent to both of the new Dominions, it could reasonably have joined either. In contrast to both Hyderabad and Junagadh, Kashmir, through an accident of history, had a Hindu ruler and a mixed population of which the majority, however, were Muslim. The crisis in Kashmir resulted in an almost symbolic military conflict between the new states of India and Pakistan. Each side claimed provocation from the other. What is clear is that, on 24 October 1947, well-armed and organized Pathan tribesmen crossed the frontier of Kashmir from Pakistan and marched on the capital Srinagar. Despite his family's Kashmiri origins, Nehru at first seemed reluctant to authorize military intervention. Lord Mountbatten, the Governor General, also hoped to avoid such drastic action.

A majority of ministers, however, strongly supported the principle of intervention. Perhaps surprisingly, Gandhi a few months before his assassination, argued forcefully that peace could not be achieved by submitting to the forces of evil in Kashmir. The Hindu ruler of Kashmir now acceded to India, and on 27 October Indian troops were flown into the province to halt the advancing irregular force. The Kashmir crisis provided a dramatic testing time for Nehru's diplomatic skill. After his early hesitation, the Prime Minister became determined not to compromise over the incorporation of the province into India. Believing that the integrity of the new India, and, paradoxically, that of Pakistan, depended on firm action over Kashmir, Nehru argued that 'we are playing for much higher stakes than might appear on the surface'.[2]

The conflict in Kashmir also put Nehru's internationalist principles to a severe test. Unwilling to accept in full a variety of United Nations proposals aimed at settling the confrontation, his Government showed its determination to protect India's interests in Kashmir to the full. This went as far as fighting a short, but fierce, war with Pakistan in Kashmir during 1948. Although a ceasefire, based on the proposals of a United Nations commission, was eventually accepted, Kashmir has remained firmly within the Indian union ever since. The promised plebiscite never took place.

It has been argued that Nehru's unrelenting stance on Kashmir was chiefly the result of an almost romantic attachment to the province of his forebears. But this is too simplistic an explanation. Nor can any real justification for India's hard line be found in the Maharajah of Kashmir's accession to India. After all, the rulers of Junagadh and Hyderabad were Muslims who had opted the other way, and their provinces had been incorporated into the Indian union. There were, however, strong practical reasons for Nehru's attitude. One was that Kashmir was a frontier province and would therefore provide some defence against possible aggression from China. The other was that the accession of a predominantly Muslim state to India was a powerful demonstration of the secular quality of the new Dominion's Government.

India's new constitution was, indeed, being finalized at the same time. The Constituent Assembly produced constitutional proposals with commendable clarity and lack of conflict. Implemented from 1950, the constitution owed a great deal to the 1935 Government of India Act, and indeed lengthy passages from the Act were incorporated within it. The continuing influence of British rule did not end there. Although the constitution established a federal state with a western parliamentary type of democracy, it was notable for the strength of central government. Just as under diarchy the Raj had been unwilling to hand over certain responsibilities to the provinces, so the centralized Government of India had sole control of defence, foreign affairs, railways, ports and currency. Moreover there was a list of 'concurrent' legislative subjects on which the centre could intervene and override the provinces. There were also reserved residuary powers at the centre. The President of the union could take over a state's administration and impose direct rule – just like the Viceroys before him. The concentration of power at the centre was to enable Nehru to push through controversial measures which were resented by particular interest groups or provinces.

The central Parliament had two chambers: the Lok Sabha, which represented the mass electorate, and the Rajya Sabha, which represented the states. Ministers were responsible, in the British tradition, to the legislature. The constitutional right of the President to intervene in affairs of state would not become an issue while a government ruled with a clear parliamentary majority, but in the event of an inconclusive general election or the shifting of political groupings within the legislature, the President's powers could become decisive. In practice, during Nehru's premiership, these problems did not arise, since Congress achieved such an overwhelming parliamentary supremacy that it was virtually obliged to provide effective opposition to government policies from within its own ranks. The new constitution also incorporated the principle of universal suffrage, giving India at independence some 175 million voters, thus making it the largest democratic electorate in the world. The constitution provided a definition of fundamental citizens' rights, almost on the American model, and also incorporated a list of constitutional directives or goals. Subsequent developments in the constitution were mostly to involve rulings of the independent Federal Court. The assertion of the fundamental rights of the individual included the abolition in theory and practice of 'untouchability' and of caste distinctions. In the event, however, it was not such a simple matter. Overall, the constitution was unashamedly based upon western political and ethical principles.

One final piece of transitional business was the ending of India's dominion status. Congress had reluctantly accepted the constitutional status of a British Dominion in order to hasten and finalize the transfer of power. Now this had been achieved, there was no reason why the Government could not press for the country to become a republic. The chief problem was one of form. India wished to remain within the Commonwealth. How was this compatible with becoming a republic? The Irish Free State had left the Commonwealth on attaining republican status; Burma had never even joined. In the event, a typically British compromise emerged. The British monarch, to whom in theory each Dominion owed allegiance, was redesignated Head of the Commonwealth. Thus future republics had merely to acknowledge this position, not owe allegiance in the way in which Australia and Canada still did. By January 1950, India had become a republic, the first of many to come within the Commonwealth.

The years 1950–56 were in many ways the heyday of Nehru's premiership. Congress, the party that had brought the country to independence, was overwhelmingly supported by the people as the decisive general election victory of 1952 demonstrated. In terms of domestic policy, however, the task which faced the administration was enormous and the solutions not easy to find. The main objective of the Nehru Government was to bring about an improvement in the standards of living of the Indian people, and to give them some tangible hope for the future. Prior to independence, Nehru had been strongly associated with socialist theory and the need for planned economic development. In office, things could not be implemented so straightforwardly. A host of factors, not least the strong capitalist framework of India's economy, had to be taken into consideration. Many interest groups demanded attention and priority treatment, and questions of timing and methods of implementation became crucial to the structuring of overall policy. In the conflict between socialist theory and capitalist realities, it was the theory that had the worst of it.

Instead of a redistribution of land and wealth, the Government placed increasing emphasis upon the need to expand production and for the prosperity thus generated to filter through to the lower orders of society.

Although Nehru's administration was committed to nationalization, it was emphasized that state ownership would only be put into effect if it did not disrupt production and unbalance existing economic structures. Progress of this kind should, in short, be gradual. Therefore the Government restricted public ownership to munitions, atomic energy and railways, and laid down markers for the future by reserving to themselves the sole right to start new industries in coal, iron and steel, aircraft manufacturing, shipbuilding, telephone and telegraph materials, and minerals. All existing industries were given the guarantee that they would not face even the prospect of nationalization for at least ten years.

As Nehru's administration moved away from putting its socialist theories into practice, it was able to gain some satisfaction from the investment of public money in the great river development schemes such as those of the Damodar Valley and the Hirakud Dam in Orissa. When, in 1949, an economic crisis forced the Government to introduce cuts in public spending, Nehru was adamant that there should be no reduction in the investment in these highly symbolic river valley projects with their capacity for bringing profound economic and social improvements.

The task of raising living standards, in which these great power and irrigation projects played such an important part, was so enormous as to appear almost impossible. Yet Nehru and his administration tackled the problems with great energy and consistency of purpose. They were not helped in their labours by the rapid rise in the nation's population. In 1951 India's population was over 356 millions. Ten years later it had risen to more than 434 millions. The Government's strategy for improving the standard of living was twofold: to increase agricultural output significantly and to encourage industrialization in order to boost production. In 1950 Nehru set up the National Planning Commission, a body with sufficient constitutional powers to enable hard decisions to be made and progress to be achieved. In 1951, the first Five-Year Plan was launched, concentrating especially upon agricultural production. At the end of the five years, Nehru and his colleagues could feel considerable satisfaction; agricultural production had risen by some 25 per cent, thus helping to free India from her over-dependence upon overseas food supplies. Considerable industrial development also took place, notably the establishment of three new steel plants, sponsored by Britain, West Germany and Russia respectively, and all operating within the public sector. The private sector's activities continued unabated at the same time. During this period the Government claimed that the national income had risen by 18 per cent, a considerable advance when set against the continuing rapid increase in the population.

The undoubted success of the first Five-Year Plan led to the launching of a second and even more ambitious and expensive plan in 1956.

Social reforms went hand in hand with economic ones. Here again, Nehru's socialist inclinations had to be tempered by expediency. It was not possible to carry through anything like the radical land reforms that were necessary to ensure India's peasantry a future free from servitude and debt. There was the abolition, in the aftermath of independence, of the *zamindari* system – the traditional, and frequently oppressive, form of landlordism and rent collection. But this reform did not eliminate landlords or replace them with rural co-operatives as Nehru hoped. In fact, with no limit set on the amount of land that an individual could own, rich tenants prospered at the expense of the middle and lower peasantry. The rural poor were still very much part of India's countryside.

Nonetheless the Community Development Programme, which Nehru passionately supported, gave to the masses an increased responsibility for improving their environment. Initially concerned with the development of amenities such as roads, schools and irrigation, Nehru hoped that the scheme could be extended to the promotion of intensive agricultural production as well. By 1956 the Community Development Programme had been extended to roughly a quarter of rural India.

It has been argued that the achievements in boosting agricultural production were being simultaneously and seriously undermined by the rapidly increasing population. A family planning programme was begun in 1950, but it aroused widespread misgivings and hostility and its implementation remained feeble. Nehru had been accused of failing to give priority to the family planning programme, and instead putting his faith unrealistically in an increase in food production, the spread of education, the establishment of a health service, and the development programme, to help solve the problem. It took him some years to realize how vital to India's future well-being an effective birth control policy would be.

Nehru encouraged a variety of important social reforms, designed to make India a more equitable and civilized society. His desire to enhance the rights of the individual was founded on his western liberal, philosophical approach. But although untouchability and the legality of caste restrictions had been abolished in the constitution, this did not automatically guarantee the individual adequate civil rights. In order to achieve this, the Nehru Government introduced important bills to amend Hindu social law, where the group had more weight than the individual and where the woman was subordinate to the man. Such policies were bound to strike at the heart of religious susceptibilities and prejudice, and it proved impossible to introduce all the reforms that the Prime Minister would ideally have wished for.

Nonetheless, by 1956 two very significant measures had been passed: the Hindu Succession Act in 1955, and the Hindu Marriage Act in 1956. The first gave women equal rights with men in matters of succession to, and in the holding of, property. The second gave monogamy a legal basis, and made provision for divorce – with the attendant side-products of alimony and maintenance. Yet another act made provision for the maintenance of Hindu widows and of separated wives. Asked, towards the end of his life, what he thought of as the greatest real piece of progress achieved under his premiership, Nehru had replied 'the measures for the improvement of the condition of Hindu women'.[3] But faced, both within Congress and without, by powerful forces that opposed such reforms, even Nehru could not secure the passing of the Hindu Code as a whole. For Muslim women he could do nothing, wary of the potentially violent response that reforms would provoke amongst India's Islamic community.

Education reform was another essential, though daunting, task. Improved rates of literacy and, at a higher level, the spread of technical education, were considered vital to India's programme of industrial and agricultural development. The constitution had directed that by 1961 every child up to the age of fourteen should enjoy free and compulsory education. This had been nowhere achieved by 1956, nor eight years later at the time of Nehru's death. Nevertheless, there was a considerable and sustained investment in primary and secondary education, and an even more successful drive to expand tertiary education, universities, colleges, technical institutes and the like. Because of the smaller scale of the problem, the proliferation of tertiary educational institutions was much more marked than the expansion of primary and secondary education. The literacy rate, a meagre 15 per cent of the population at independence, climbed slowly but steadily.

One of Nehru's major domestic problems arose from Congress's long-standing commitment to the creation of provinces on a linguistic basis. Once in power, the Nehru Government gave the matter low priority until an eruption of agitation and protest brought the matter sharply to their attention during 1955. The agitation was provoked by the publication of the report of the commission working on the issue of a reorganization of the country's provincial governments. The report provoked a torrent of protest and threatened to open up a multitude of linguistic and provincial rivalries and animosities. Anxious not to antagonize provincial sentiment, the Government for some time appeared to dither over the issue. Some of the most vehement objections came from the Punjab, where the Sikh community wanted its own state, and from Bombay city and the surrounding Marathi-speaking districts, whose people demanded a separate state, Maharashtra, rather than being linked with the other major provincial group, the Gujaratis, in a bilingual state. Rioting and a considerable number of deaths resulted from the agitation. After unsatisfactory and temporary compromises over Bombay, the official reorganization of India's states had taken place by the end of 1956. The story was not, however, to end here and further rearrangements were inevitable.

Linked to the demand for linguistic provinces was the whole fraught issue of the official language of the new India. Nehru was prepared to go along with the demand that Hindi should be made the official language, although he expressed disquiet at the potential hostility that this would produce, particularly in the south of the country. However, he also wished to retain English alongside Hindi, thus precipitating a lengthy controversy between himself and his supporters and the enthusiasts for the supremacy of Hindi. It gave Nehru no comfort to see his predictions fulfilled, and an increasing amount of resentment expressed at the elevation of Hindi to the status of the official language.

Despite the undoubted domestic successes that his Government had achieved, the scale of the problems that presented themselves meant that Nehru turned with increasing relief and satisfaction to matters of foreign policy. Here he achieved, within a short space of time, an international status, unique amongst contemporary statesmen. Nehru strove to ensure that India pursued a policy of non-alignment during the Cold War. This was not always easy, as the confused Indian reaction to the outbreak of the Korean War in 1950 showed. Although India's representative at the United Nations, B. N. Rau, voted on his own initiative for the Security Council resolution of 25 June condemning the North Korean invasion of the South and calling upon UN members to work for the cessation of hostilities and the withdrawal of the North's forces to the 38th parallel, Delhi directed him to make no further commitment without prior consultation. The Nehru Government then proceeded to sit on the fence: it accepted a second United Nation's resolution of 27 June directing member states to give assistance to South Korea, but did not provide any military support to this end. Nehru's policy, not one designed to please Washington or London, was expressed succinctly in a communication to B. N. Rau on 1 July 1950: 'Our moral help is a big enough thing, which out-balances the petty military help of some other countries.'[4]

In general, however, Nehru was careful to affirm that non-alignment did not imply indifference: 'Where freedom is menaced or justice threatened or where aggression takes place, we cannot be and shall not be neutral.'[5] Although many critics observed that, in practice, this policy was variable, and that Nehru was overall more sympathetic to the west, others have argued that he genuinely believed the western powers to be more culpable than the communist bloc on issues such as racialism and colonialism. In the last resort, Nehru, from deep conviction, and by political instinct, was hostile to totalitarianism, and this, plus the potential threat from China, decisively coloured his attitude towards communism.

On the international stage, at the United Nations, or at Commonwealth Conferences, Nehru cut an imposing figure. Here he frequently denounced what he saw as colonialism. Thus he supported the ejection of the Dutch from Indonesia, and of the French from Indo-China. When in November 1956 Britain and France invaded Egypt during the Suez crisis, and at the same time the Soviet Union crushed the Hungarian uprising, Nehru saved his most bitter denunciations for the Anglo-French aggression. In the same vein he tried to tidy up India's colonial remnants, welcoming the early French withdrawal from their small territorial enclaves, but growing increasingly inpatient that Portugal was refusing to withdraw from Goa.

For a while, Nehru aspired to the moral leadership of Asia. His strong support for, and participation in, the Bandung Conference of 1955 was symbolic of this intent. Held at Bandung, in Indonesia, in April 1955, the Conference brought together twenty-nine Afro-Asian nations to discuss interests of common concern and to assert their independent identities. Nehru played a dominant part in the proceedings, and later told the Indian Parliament that 'Bandung proclaimed the political emergence in world affairs of over half the world's population'. But apart from sending a warning, especially to the western powers, that there could be no return to colonialism or dependency, the Bandung Conference achieved nothing by way of a permanent organization. It had made a gesture and shown some defiance for the old world order, but that was about all. In practice Asianism, like Africanism, was a fragile and nebulous concept, and in any case would somehow have to accommodate the expanding power of China. Nehru did his best to head off any potential difficulties in the latter area by going out of his way to cultivate good relations with the Chinese communist authorities, and agreeing with them five principles of co-existence in 1954.

Non-alignment was not simply based upon some high-principled, Gandhian philosophy of non-violence and peace. If India was to promote internal development and prosperity, it could simply not afford the vast expenditure on armaments which active support of either side in the Cold War implied. Moreover, Nehru feared that the forging of military alliances and treaties of mutual aid could well disguise a covert return of western, or Soviet, imperialism. Despite the high moral tone that often marked Nehru's speeches on international matters, to the frequent annoyance of foreign statesmen, he was preaching a practical message. If India could demonstrate the success of non-alignment, this could be to the advantage of other emerging nations and to the cause of world peace.

Naturally, his stand caused bitter resentment in some quarters. The United States Government was resentful of his refusal to brand China as an aggressor during the Korean war. And it was not until the end of 1956 and the Suez crisis, on which America and India found themselves in accord, that relations improved. Doubtless the need for United States aid had much to do with it. Nehru now spoke in public of American support for India's struggle for freedom, and made this appeal during a visit to the United States: 'We wish to learn from you and we plead for your friendship, co-operation and sympathy in the great task we have undertaken in our country.'[6]

As 1956 drew to its close, Nehru seemed to enjoy unrivalled supremacy at home and almost universal respect abroad. But, while his capacity for influencing events on the world stage was necessarily limited, within India it is true to say that every area of policy was supervised and frequently determined by him. He could bring Congress to heel with a hint of resignation. Dissent in Cabinet was rare, but could be quelled with a firm word or even a bang on the table with his hand. He stood for a pluralist democracy, from the enfranchisement of tens of millions of low-caste and untouchable Hindus, to the village committees or *panchayats* which he was instrumental in reviving; from the mobilizing of the largest democratic mass electorate in the world to the successful functioning of provincial legislatures. He played a vital part in ensuring the vitality of Parliament by carrying out his duties as leader of the Lok Sabha, and of the Congress Party in that chamber, with commitment and consistency. Through his regular parliamentary attendance, his answering of Prime Minister's questions and his skilful use of his abilities in debate, he helped to entrench the parliamentary system within the new India.

He had his failures. Too much autonomy was allowed to some party bosses in the provinces, and corruption was never eliminated. Even within Congress, there were substantial elements within the right wing of the party that obstructed, even if passively, much of his reforming programme.

Poverty, hopelessness and suffering were still too commonly the lot of the Indian people. But the local communist threat had been contained and the clamour for linguistic provinces largely satisfied.

All Nehru's long-term goals, including planned development, social justice, popular democracy, increasing economic self-reliance, and the promotion of India as a non-aligned and respected member of the international community, still seemed attainable.

9
Final Years and Mounting Problems 1956–1964

Nehru's last eight years as Prime Minister were marked by a proliferation of problems, both domestic and external, which provided him with some of the greatest trials and setbacks of his career. It has been claimed that Nehru's failure to take a firmer grip on events, particularly in domestic policy, and especially his unwillingness to abandon or at least modify a fundamentally democratic mode of operation, made the tackling of a variety of problems far more difficult, if not impossible.

A desire to promote economic development through state planning was central to Nehru's philosophy. India's second Five-Year Plan was initiated in 1956. It was even more ambitious than the first, and put even more emphasis on the development of heavy industry and machine building; for example, providing for an annual increase in steel production from one and a half million tons to six million tons per annum. But since only a quarter of the necessary finance for the plan could be guaranteed from government revenue, the remainder had to come from loans, deficit financing and foreign aid. This, in turn, meant that the Indian economy became increasingly dependent upon the goodwill of international institutions such as the World Bank and upon aid from richer and friendly countries. One clear implication of this increasing dependency was that the country's foreign policy could no longer aspire to the generally independent and non-aligned quality of the first years following independence.

Successful industrial expansion, however, needed a strong and developing agricultural base in order to feed a fast-growing population and to provide reasonably stable food prices. Here Nehru hoped that the promotion of co-operative farming, allied with the extension of the

Community Development Programme, would provide the answer. By 1956 the Community Development Programme had already spread to nearly half of India's villages, and it was planned to extend its activities to the rest of the country over the next five years. The programme was meant to inspire and train large numbers of the rural population to carry out improvements in agricultural production, to organize the building of roads, schools and hospitals, and to promote cottage and small-scale industries.

Economic development and rural co-operation would lead, Nehru still hoped, to the development of a socialist society in India. There was a great deal of confusion and contradiction, however, about what form India's socialism would take. Despite the commitment to planning, and the expansion of the public sector, private enterprise continued to flourish and was, indeed, essential to economic success. Nehru seems to have been thinking of a peculiarly Indian form of socialism, compatible with deep national and cultural traditions, and developing slowly and pragmatically. Crucial to his philosophy was a commitment not merely to a programme of economic development, but to a popular revolution in attitudes which would help refashion society in a progressive way.[1] There was no doubting the democratic flavour of this approach, but it was imprecise, over-optimistic, and almost certain to fail.

Within a year, the second Five-Year Plan had been seriously disrupted by unfavourable weather conditions – floods, storms, and drought. The failure of the harvest precipitated such a serious food crisis that valuable reserves of foreign currency were used up to save the situation. This, in turn, meant that it became increasingly difficult to purchase equipment from abroad to promote industrial expansion. For a while the Government banned imports that required foreign exchange unless the providers were prepared to accept a delay in payment. The Soviet Union and other east European powers quickly agreed to this, and the principle of non-alignment was as a result put under serious threat. The situation was balanced, however, by western nations following the communist lead. At the same time, the Indian consumer market was hard hit by new taxes raised on certain goods, while the poorer sections of society suffered from a lowering of the threshold level of income tax.

The second Five-Year Plan failed to reach most of its targets. Each year larger quantities of grain were imported to feed the population, and this established policy had the further effect of increasing dependence on foreign aid and loans. The third Five-Year Plan was due to start in 1960. Two years before that date, Nehru was still sufficiently optimistic to believe that India was gradually making a success of economic planning. At least, he argued, there could be no turning back. But in practice the Government's control over the economy was far less than in the Soviet bloc, and less, even, than in the United States. Could India follow the successful path between the extremes of capitalism and communism? In November 1958, Nehru told the deputy chairman of the Planning Commission, 'I do not myself see where socialism comes in the present policies that we are pursuing. It is true that we have some major industries in the public sector. That is hardly socialism.'

Despite the increased emphasis placed upon co-operative farming during the third Five-Year Plan, nobody could pretend that India's economic and social problems had been solved. How far was Nehru responsible for these failures? His early passion for heavy industrial development can be seen as ill-judged and self-indulgent. Not until it was nearly too late did Nehru really wake up to the fact that food production held the key to economic and national progress. By then the trend of increasing reliance upon foreign imports was already well established. Above all, there was an embarrassing gap between declared government policy and its implementation. Much of the responsibility for this rests with the lethargy and corruption of the political élites in the states, who siphoned off funds intended for economic development to their own advantage, and who frequently blocked the implementation of social legislation that was designed to create a fairer and more democratic society.

Although Nehru could personally not be charged with corruption, his failure to root out the disease at lower levels of the administration was a singular failure. This reluctance to take provincial governments by the scruff of the neck and to force them to carry out government policy not only had its roots in Nehru's attachment to the democratic process, but also reflected the increasingly fragile state of the Congress political alliance. Although Congress convincingly won the general election of 1957, in the aftermath of victory Nehru told his party leadership, 'You know well enough how poisoned we are to the very core'.

Nehru's inability to match the idealistic aims of his administration with the achievement of these ideals gave comfort to his political enemies and an atmosphere of increasing unreality to his premiership. Each year, Congress would endorse more radical policies, and simultaneously become more reactionary and obstructive. The widespread cynicism and despair which resulted from this process also helped to discourage the reformers within Congress and cast a shadow over Nehru's own integrity. If the Prime Minister could not, literally, deliver the goods, why should he be venerated and sustained?

One spectacular result of the increasing discontent with Congress rule was the victory of the Communist party in the southern state of Kerala in the 1957 elections. In contrast to the local Congress party, the Communists had established over several years a reputation for honesty and integrity. Initially, Nehru sought for the means of co-operating with the administration in Kerala, but conflict was unavoidable. Inspired partly by local Congress agitators, civil disorder and confusion became endemic to the scene in Kerala. After considerable hesitation, and with some misgivings, Nehru eventually dismissed the administration led by E. M. S. Namboodiripad, and took over the administration. The Prime Minister was well aware of the unfortunate precedent which this act set, reminiscent of the British Raj at its most autocratic. But he argued that the fateful decision had been 'hurled upon us by circumstances'. Although he had acted decisively, this gave him little personal pleasure.

In almost the opposite corner of the country, in the far north-east, the tribesmen of the Naga hills were demanding independence from the Indian union. Under the British, the Nagas had generally escaped the heavy hand of the administration and had avoided integration with the rest of the Indian community. European missionary activity had been particularly effective in the area, and many Nagas were Christians, thus giving the crisis a religious edge. At the time of independence the Nagas had been promised, by Nehru and others, an exceptional degree of local autonomy. In the early 1950s, however, the Nagas began to demand independence from the Government of Assam and from India itself.

Nehru visited the Naga hills in 1952 and frankly told the dissidents that there was no chance of independence, but that he was prepared to help them maintain their individuality in cultural and other matters. He also hoped that, with benevolent administration and through the improvement of the standard of living in the area, the Nagas would consider themselves to be in partnership with, not in opposition to, central and local government. The strategy, though, failed, and an armed uprising ensued. By the spring of 1956 the Indian Army had been sent into the Naga hills to restore order. At the same time Nehru promised the rebels an amnesty and the maximum autonomy compatible with remaining within the national state. His conciliatory attitude was viewed as weakness in some quarters, and unfortunately did not bring Naga resistance to an end.

By 1960 the situation had still not been resolved. In a bid to break the deadlock, Nehru conceded the creation of a state of Nagaland within the Indian Union. For a while, a settlement seemed possible, but a year later the army and the Naga tribesmen were still in conflict. No permanent solution had been found to the problem by the time of Nehru's death in May 1964, although amongst his last initiatives was the sending of a mission to Nagaland to negotiate a settlement. He may have drawn some satisfaction from the signing of a preliminary agreement a few days before he died, but the Naga uprising was one problem, among many, that he was unable to solve.

The difficulties of dealing with a host of other linguistic, communal and religious differences were manifold. In practice it proved impossible to guarantee freedom from persecution and harassment to many minority groups; the dream of a well-ordered, tolerant pluralistic society was never to be realized. Muslims, for example, were the victims of communal assault by the Hindu majority in the provinces of Bihar, Madhya Pradesh and Uttar Pradesh during the spring and early summer of 1959. In February 1961 there was a renewal of serious communal violence in Madhya Pradesh. Muslims in the city of Jabalpur protested at the attitude of the Hindu-dominated police force in the province. Nehru was convinced that the communal riots had been carefully organized by Hindu extremists, and ordered the Chief Minister of Madhya Pradesh to deal with the troublemakers under the Preventive Detention Act if need be. Although the Prime Minister gave testimony on numerous occasions to his strong commitment to pluralism and secularism, the increasing politicization of conflicts over religion, caste and language was an increasingly troublesome and depressing phenomenon.

Nehru was prepared to make some compromises to promote national harmony. The general election results of 1957 had revealed that the earlier decision to maintain Bombay as a bilingual province was deeply unpopular in both Maharashtra and Gujarat. Rioting had occurred in Ahmedabad, and the police had opened fire on the crowds. Bowing to sustained pressure from the province and from groups within Congress, in 1960 Nehru reluctantly sanctioned the splitting of the old province of Bombay into two new states, Maharashtra and Gujarat. Thus by 1961 the map of provincial India had been substantially redrawn from the days of the Raj.

The debate over the use of Hindi and English as official languages also rumbled on. Although the decision had been taken in principle gradually to promote Hindi as the language of administration and education, the clamour for the redrawing of state boundaries based on linguistic differences, and the determination of minorities to maintain their identities, made a complex situation even more complicated. It would have been self-destructive to have forced Hindi on provinces where the regional language was not merely preferred but also increasing in usage. Then there was the position of English. Nehru believed that English should continue to be taught and its usage encouraged as an additional all-Indian language. Despite the association of English with the era of British rule, and with an Indian educational élite, there were clear advantages in continuing to promote its use.

Compromise and prevarication marked the debate over a national language. Although the constitution had prescribed that Hindi should be gradually established as the official language of the Indian Union, by 1959 Nehru had felt it necessary to promise that there would be no imposition of this policy, and that English would survive as an additional, official language for the foreseeable future. In the last resort, of course, Hindi could only be accepted as the national language with provincial consent. The rather messy compromise over language was put into legislative form in the Official Languages Act of 1963. This measure stated that English 'may' continue to be used after 1965, as well as Hindi, for the official business of the nation and parliament. Inevitably this compromise did not settle the problem, and it was to pass, along with many others, to those who succeeded to the premiership after Nehru.

Quite apart from the controversy over the official language, there was the problem of the continuing usage of Urdu. Nehru was insistent that Urdu, a language recognized by the constitution and used by India's substantial Muslim minority, should be allowed its proper place in a pluralistic society. The danger, however, of promoting Urdu was that it might inflame communal hatreds and provide Hindu fundamentalists with more sticks with which to beat the Government. On the other hand, how could India's Muslims feel reconciled to their position within the Indian Union if their language was discouraged rather than encouraged? Nehru, who spoke Urdu himself, felt strongly enough on the issue to instruct the Chief Minister of Uttar Pradesh to promote the usage of Urdu, and several times brought the whole issue before the Cabinet. From these discussions another woolly compromise emerged, whereby a bland statement was issued asserting that all languages should be encouraged as far as possible and in a spirit of tolerance and communal friendship. As with so many other matters, however, there was a substantial difference between theory and practice.

If the problems of communalism, provincialism and language usage formed a quagmire into which Nehru sank deeper and deeper as his premiership drew to a close, he could at least claim some success in the tidying up of various geographical left-overs from India's colonial past. Although the French had left the sub-continent by 1954, the Portuguese had not. Portugal was to remain one of the most unrepentant of the western colonial powers, and her government one of the most reactionary in Europe, for a considerable time. In 1961, Nehru's patience with the Portuguese authorities evaporated, and on 18 December Indian forces invaded Goa and incorporated it into the Indian Union. The use of force in this instance was in embarrassing contrast to Nehru's world stance as a statesman dedicated to internationalism. In the United States, and elsewhere, the Prime Minister was accused of hypocrisy after his numerous appearances on the world stage lecturing his listeners on the importance of a non-violent approach to international disputes and controversies. Nehru defended his action in Goa by arguing that, as the Portuguese had not resisted the invasion, it could be considered a non-violent act. Despite support from the Soviet Union and many non-aligned nations, this sort of defence cut little ice elsewhere. Nehru bitterly resented the criticism which was levelled at him, but his international image remained somewhat tarnished thereafter.

One of the reasons why such firm action was taken over Goa was undoubtedly the need to demonstrate that India would resort to military force in certain situations. A clear warning was thus sent, both explicitly and implicitly, to China with whom India was entangled in an increasingly bitter dispute over border areas. Nehru was asked at a press conference shortly after the Goa invasion whether India was now prepared to use force against China, and replied, 'The use of force is of course open to us and should be used according to suitability and opportunity.' The success of the incorporation of Goa into the new India, and the apparent readiness of the Government to fight the Chinese if they did not withdraw from occupied border areas, was used to great effect during the general election of 1962.

Early in 1962 Nehru led his party into the third and, as it happened, the last general election of his premiership. The incorporation of Goa into the Indian Union had boosted morale, just as the continuing military threat from China on the northern borders helped to consolidate national feeling. Indeed, Government ministers continued to make a direct connection between Goa and the Chinese threat. As we have seen, Nehru had already made it plain that he did not rule out the use of force against China, and one of his ministers Lal Bahadur Shastri asserted, while campaigning, that 'If the Chinese will not vacate the areas occupied by her, India will have to repeat what she did in Goa.'[3]

Despite losing twenty three-seats in the central Parliament, Congress won a substantial victory in the election of 1962. Doubtless the Goa factor counted for a lot, as did the continuing potency of Nehru's appeal to the electorate. Although Congress maintained its overwhelming hold on the centre of Indian politics and carried nearly all the states, the extreme left and right-wing parties made considerable advances. Nehru was relatively philosophical about the successes of the Communist party, which seemed to him at least to have a coherent set of ideals, despite its tendency to take instructions from Moscow. He reserved his most outspoken criticism for right-wing parties like the Hindu Fundamentalist Jan Sangh, and Swatantra which he regarded as possessing the 'bullock-cart mentality'.[4]

Although Congress had triumphed yet again in the general election, it might have fared far worse if the truth had been revealed about India's military unpreparedness in the face of Chinese aggression on the border. There were serious shortages of equipment, even of such essentials as boots. Nehru threw his political weight behind the Minister for Defence, Krishna Menon, during the election campaigning. He claimed that the army was a strong and effective fighting force whereas in reality its weaknesses were soon to be revealed. Part of the responsibility for the military humiliations which were to come belonged to Nehru, who as Prime Minister presided over a Cabinet where ministers could sometimes pursue policies without properly informing him, or present him with *faits accomplis* that he was obliged to accept.

Something else was kept from the electorate. Nehru's health was failing, and after the election campaign he became quite seriously ill with a debilitating kidney disease, pyelonephritis. The official explanation of his illness was that he was suffering from overwork, and later, after a thoroughgoing medical examination in London, he was declared to be in excellent health. But this is not how it appeared to those who saw him in the flesh. He had developed a slight stoop, and was beginning to slow down. He was, after all, now in his seventy-second year. Inevitably, Nehru's deteriorating health prompted speculation over who would eventually succeed him as Prime Minister. This problem, however, assumed an insignificance in the face of the dramatic and bloody military confrontation with China.

The Communist Government of China had come to power in 1949, two years after India had won independence. Both of these huge countries aspired to, at least, the moral leadership of Asia. As Prime Minister, Nehru had done his best to cultivate a good and harmonious relationship with China. When the Chinese had invaded Tibet in 1950, claiming it as part of their historical territory, India had accepted the fact with as good grace as possible. In fact, it made little sense for the Government of India to continue the quasi-imperial policies of the British Raj towards Tibet. On the other hand, Nehru was insistent that the north-east frontier between India and Tibet established in 1913, and known as the McMahon line, was fixed and not open to negotiation. But circumstances had changed since the heyday of British rule. Then China had been a weak and disunited country, while the Raj had been able to assert its interests on its northern frontiers and build up a number of buffer states, like Nepal and Bhutan and, less formally, Tibet. By 1950, however, China was a reconstituted, self-confident and expanding power, while India was preaching co-existence and non-aggression.

In 1954, Nehru made a bid to put Indian–Chinese relations on to a permanent and friendly footing. He visited the People's Republic, and was generally impressed with what he saw. Out of this visit came the 1954 agreement incorporating five principles of co-existence between the two countries. In political terms, India accepted the occupation of Tibet, while China made no formal claims for a redrawing of the frontier. This situation, however, was unlikely to last.

For one thing, Nehru was over-optimistic that the 1954 agreement represented a permanent acceptance by China of the northern frontier. Even though the Chinese had raised no objections to the McMahon line, at the western end of the frontier no such line was drawn on a map. The British had not properly surveyed the area, and had not laid down any clear frontier lines. But Nehru persisted in claiming that the northern frontier was fixed, and proceeded to establish checkposts along the whole border. Finding their protests ignored, the Chinese began to build a road through the desolate, western end of the frontier, known as the Aksai Chin. The Indian Government did not become aware of this activity until 1957. Several border incidents occurred, but Nehru, who was becoming increasingly secretive and arbitrary over the conduct of foreign policy, kept many of the details not merely from the Indian public, but also from his cabinet colleagues. Eventually in October 1958, India protested to Peking over the construction of the road through Aksai Chin. Relations between the two countries began rapidly to deteriorate, and Nehru persisted in rejecting the reasonable diplomatic overtures of the Chinese Prime Minister, Chou Enlai. Such inflexibility was imprudent on two counts. One was that Nehru was painting himself into a corner, giving India very little room for manoeuvre. The other was that India's military strength was quite inadequate to underpin so unbending an attitude.

During 1959 Sino-Indian relations reached a nadir with the arrival in the sub-continent of the Tibetan religious leader the Dalai Lama. The Dalai Lama had fled to India following his public support for a Tibetan rebellion against Chinese rule. Although Nehru tried to placate the Peking Government, the Chinese attacked him for 'walking in the footsteps of the British imperialists and harbouring expansionist ambitions towards Tibet'.[5] Over the next three years, the situation deteriorated steadily, resulting in the final tragedy of a full military confrontation in 1962. It seems clear that it was India who during these years rejected Chinese overtures for a peaceful settlement, and continued to push troops into disputed areas, particularly on the western frontier. The People's Republic had indicated on several occasions that it would be prepared to settle for the cession of the Aksai Chin, but Nehru rejected the proposal out of hand. The Prime Minister's attitude was based on a number of miscalculations, including the belief that China would not, in the last resort, attack India, and by a foolishly misplaced faith in the efficiency of the Indian armed services.

In October 1962 the Chinese, running out of patience, carried out a full-scale assault along the frontier, particularly in the west. Within a month, Chinese successes had destroyed forever the Indian assumption of military superiority. The débâcle on the northern frontier precipitated a political crisis, leaving Nehru exposed as an old and dispirited leader. India was saved from further humiliation by the Chinese unilateral ceasefire at the end of November 1962, and by the continuing insistence of the Peking Government that it wished to negotiate a reasonable solution.

The war on the northern frontier also had the effect of tarnishing Nehru's image as a non-aligned leader. The Russian Government, bitterly at odds with their fellow-communists at Peking, increased both economic and military aid to India. But the greatest embarrassment for Nehru arose from his need to appeal to the United States for assistance. When the cease-fire was declared, an American aircraft-carrier was on its way to the Bay of Bengal. American transport planes flew supplies to the troops at the frontier. Both the United States and Britain sent high-ranking personnel to India to assist in the modernization of the armed forces. It is also clear that the Americans offered to supply necessary air cover in the event of another Chinese assault. The taking of aid from both the Soviet Union and the west did not deflect criticism that, in the final analysis, Nehru's and India's neutrality was of a pro-western variety. The dispute with China had not been resolved by the time of Nehru's death.

The inconveniences of India's failure to remain truly non-aligned were soon made evident. The United States and Britain both made demands that in return for their military assistance against the Chinese threat, they expected a settlement of the long-running dispute with Pakistan over

Kashmir. Shortly after the cease-fire at the end of November 1962 it was announced that Nehru would meet the President of Pakistan, Ayub Khan, to explore a possible solution to the Kashmir problem. Nothing came of this meeting, however, and Nehru was promptly declaring before the Indian Parliament that he would never be willing to 'upset the present arrangement in Kashmir'. Subsequent talks at a lower level finally petered out, and the confrontation over Kashmir seemed as far from a solution as ever. Nehru's intransigence on this issue had deep roots, but was also possibly based on the calculation that American support would continue even if he continued to defy them on the issue of a settlement in Kashmir. At any rate, Kashmir remained part of the Indian Union.

The humiliation of India's military failure on the northern frontier, and the growing and potentially awkward dependence upon western support, should not be allowed to disguise Nehru's real successes on the international stage. For one thing, he was a founder-member of the new Commonwealth, and was instrumental in helping that disparate and ill-defined group of nations toward a rational and honourable evolution. This did not prevent family quarrels from taking place, and Nehru could be outspoken in his criticism of Britain, as for instance in the case of the Suez affair of 1956-7. But the Commonwealth could not survive unless its member nations felt free to express their opinions in this fashion, and Nehru's skill in sticking to his principles, voicing objections at Britain's policy, and yet keeping India in the 'club', was of enormous benefit. Many saw him in the aftermath of Suez as quite simply the saviour of the new Commonwealth. He was, however, sometimes pushed to the brink of disillusionment, as for example over the attitudes of some Commonwealth countries towards South Africa and its policy of apartheid. When South Africa opted for republican status, and then applied for continuing membership of the Commonwealth in 1961, Nehru was resolutely opposed to the proposal. He made it plain that the Commonwealth stood in danger of disintegration if the policy of apartheid was to be tolerated in a member nation. Faced with predominantly Afro-Asian opposition, orchestrated in large part by Nehru, South Africa decided to withdraw its application for continuing membership. Privately, Nehru had indicated that if the Pretoria Government were to be accommodated within the Commonwealth he would seriously consider withdrawing India from the organization.

Elsewhere, Nehru's standing as the leader of a large and theoretically non-aligned Asian country enabled him to make unique contributions to the solving of international problems. When he spoke on issues as diverse as the crisis in the Congo or the war in Vietnam, his words carried weight even though they might also arouse indignation and fury. Nehru also moved easily through the élite ranks of world leaders, enjoying good relationships with figures as divergent as President Kennedy and Nikita Khrushchev. He was equally at his ease at Buckingham Palace or when speaking in a debate at the Oxford Union. Few doors were barred to him, and his personal charm and accessibility were widely acknowledged.

For the last two years of his life, Nehru was clearly a man whose once prodigious powers and energies were failing. The military fiasco on the northern frontier was matched by an increasing number of disappointments and frustrations at home. The Prime Minister became the object of bitter personal attacks in Parliament and there was talk in the summer of 1963 of moving a no-confidence motion against him. The challenges to Nehru's leadership were given further stimulus by a number of by-election defeats for the Congress party. A special session of the All India Congress Committee was convened to discuss the recent electoral failures and the shortcomings of the party machine. To many it also seemed that Nehru's days of power were numbered, and that a successor must be found as a matter of some urgency. Nehru even went so far as to offer his resignation, but this was inevitably refused. It became evident that the next person chosen to be President of Congress would in all probability succeed to the premiership. Out of the discussion and debate emerged a consensus that the most suitable candidate was Lal Bahadur Shastri. There were also those who lobbied on behalf of Nehru's daughter, Indira Gandhi. On his part, Nehru seems to have felt some reluctance to back Shastri. In the event, the latter did not succeed to the Congress presidency, which went instead to K. Kamaraj.

The uncertainty was eventually ended by a chance of fate. On 8 January 1964, Nehru suffered a severe stroke which paralysed his left side. Pressure was put upon the stricken Prime Minister to recall Shastri to the Cabinet. Although influential Congress leaders opposed this move, on 22 January Shastri returned to the administration as Minister without Portfolio to 'perform such functions in relation to the Ministry of External Affairs, the Department of Atomic Energy and the Cabinet Secretariat as may be assigned to him by the Prime Minister from time to time'. Despite Nehru's unwillingness to name Shastri as deputy premier, it was now accepted by many that he was in effect the chosen successor.

Although he could now have resigned with honour, Nehru chose not to do so. By the end of January 1964, it was announced that he had made a complete recovery. This was not true, as was demonstrated when he made his first visit to Parliament on 10 February. All who saw him noticed that he was still paralysed, dragged his foot and was forced to speak sitting down, finding articulation difficult. Despite this, he seemed determined to struggle on. At the end of March he announced that he would not appoint a Deputy Prime Minister. A month later he said that if he were to nominate somebody for that post it would be the surest way of his not becoming Prime Minister. At the same time he denied that he was grooming his daughter for the succession.

In a last bid to recover his health, Nehru allowed himself to be treated by practitioners of the ancient Hindu method of homeopathy, Ayurveda. Throughout the country prayers were said for him and magical rites carried out. Nehru had always treated astrology with disdain, although recognizing that many of his ministers had put much faith in the art. It is, therefore, ironical that an astrologer had warned the Prime Minister that he would suffer a serious illness in January 1964 and that he would not survive beyond 27 May. In the middle of May, Nehru seemed to be in much better health, and many Congress leaders were reassured. But a few days later, at a press conference, he once more appeared to be stricken and was only able to answer questions with a slow deliberation. After a short holiday at his favourite hill resort of Dehra Dun, the Prime Minister returned to New Delhi on 26 May.

At roughly 2 a.m. on 27 May, Nehru awoke and requested a sedative. Two hours later he woke once more in considerable pain. His discomfort increased, and finally the doctors were called and discovered at 6.45 a.m. that his aorta had ruptured and that death was imminent. Nehru lost consciousness and died at 1.44 p.m. Although he had refrained from making the decision public and final, it was widely assumed that he would be succeeded by Shastri. A new era in India's history was apparently about to begin.

Huge crowds assembled in Delhi for Nehru's funeral, lining the route taken by his cortège in their millions. After a journey of three hours, on one of the hottest days of the year, Nehru's body was laid on a five-foot-high pyre on the banks of the Jumna next to Mahatma Ghandi's last resting place. After Indira Gandhi had sprinkled holy water on the pyre and placed a piece of sandalwood at her dead father's feet, her eldest son, Sanjay, lit the flames. Countless voices joined in a final homage to India's first Prime Minister – 'Jawaharlal Nehru is immortal' – as his corpse was consumed by the fire.

Nehru's ashes were later scattered from Indian Air Force planes over Kashmir, the Himalayas, and the broad sweep of the country 'where the peasants of India toil'. But a handful was also cast into the Ganga (Ganges) at Allahabad, 'to be carried to the great ocean that washes India's shore'. Nehru had been quite specific in his will, written in June 1954, as to the disposal of his ashes, expressing himself in terms that, in a way, encapsulated the dilemmas, beliefs and contradictions of his life:

> My desire to have a handful of my ashes thrown into the Ganga at Allahabad has no religious significance, so far as I am concerned. I have no religious sentiment in this matter. I have been attached to the Ganga and Jumna rivers in Allahabad ever since my childhood and, as I have grown older, this attachment has grown... The Ganga, especially, is the river of India... She has been a symbol of India's age-long culture and civilization, ever-changing, ever-flowing, and yet ever the same... She reminds me of the snow-covered peaks and the deep valleys of the Himalayas which I have loved so much, and of the rich and vast plains below, where my life and work have been cast... And although I have discarded much of past tradition and custom, and am anxious that India should rid herself of all shackles that bind and constrain her and divide her people, and suppress vast numbers of them... though I seek all this, yet I do not wish to cut myself off from that past completely.... I am conscious that I too, like all of us, am a link in that unbroken chain which goes back to the dawn of history in the immemorial past of India; that chain I would not break, for I treasure it and seek inspiration from it.[6]

10
Nehru's Legacy

In the years since his death, Nehru's reputation has endured a harsh buffeting – a predictable fate, perhaps, for one who had aspired to greatness and exercised power on so wide a scale and for so many years. At all events, it has been possible to portray him as a man of straw, a word-smith of often dazzling virtuosity, whose actions fell tragically short of his avowed intentions.

Certainly Nehru's shortcomings as an administrator and leader were cruelly exposed by the demands of his premiership and by the intractable problems facing an independent India. His love of ideas, and his capacity for self-doubt, led to a tendency to agonize in public over the manifold choices that confronted him. His supporters saw his hesitations as proof of open-mindedness and of a dedication to democracy. His enemies dismissed his waverings as an indication of his intrinsic weakness and of a preference for inactivity in the face of daunting obstacles.

It is easy enough to construct a damning case against Nehru on a wide variety of counts. He believed in pluralism and in promoting the toleration of minorities and underdogs. But, in practice, he mostly failed to deliver, shying away, for example, from any serious attempt to advance the rights of Muslim women, and surrendering too easily to the obstructiveness of local administrations and pressure groups. His assertion in 1956 that 'untouchability' had virtually gone, was astonishing at the time and even more ludicrous in hindsight. His public dedication to socialism and economic planning was based on deep conviction and on a mature consideration, but fell far short of implementation. Big business flourished virtually unchecked, and the capitalist ethic, despite his three Five-Year Plans, remained deeply embedded in the national psyche. In the mixed economy, which Nehru was soon obliged to recognize, socialist planning and state control were distinctly poor relations.

Even if Nehru's frequently reiterated dedication to the democratic process is accepted at face value, his actions often belied his pronouncements. The intervention in Kerala, the dismissal, albeit kindly, of Naga separatism, the capacity of central government to act in as high-handed a manner as the British Raj, were all contra-indications. There were even those who saw Nehru as a quasi-viceregal figure, a brown-skinned Englishman, and thus an entirely appropriate successor to his close friend, the last Viceroy, Lord Mountbatten. An education at Harrow and Cambridge, not to speak of the influence of Harold Laski and the British Labour party, had all left permanent marks which could, far too often, become handicaps.

Nehru can thus be portrayed as a disabled Prime Minister, if not a disabled leader of Indian nationalism. The crux of the matter is whether this disability sprang from his personal failings, or from the impossibility of making real progress in the gigantic task of modernizing India and achieving a substantial improvement in the living conditions of its people. The record of those who have succeeded Nehru to the premiership, however, should perhaps give some pause to his critics.

Can an equally damning case be made by Nehru's critics in regard to India's external affairs? Here, again, there is plenty of ammunition to hand. Although Nehru led the fight against imperialism and fascism with great commitment, and at considerable personal cost, in the years prior to independence, how good was his record as a Prime Minister dedicated to non-alignment and the promotion of the interests of developing countries?

It was one thing to be a sharp critic of the Anglo-French attack upon Egypt during the Suez Crisis, or of apartheid in South Africa, or even of America's anti-communist crusading zeal. Did such posturing advance India's interest? Did lectures from the centre of the world stage put food into the mouths of the deprived, or make potentially hostile powers wary of crossing India's path? Was Nehru's international prestige merely a fig-leaf to hide his and his country's nakedness?

Worse, was Nehru essentially a hypocrite? The supporter of the United Nations who refused to consider giving up Kashmir? The sower of the seeds of a chronic and unnecessary conflict with Pakistan? The apostle of non-alignment who was never more comfortable than in communion with the powerful élites of Washington and London? The independent statesman who became increasingly dependent upon the west? The powerful leader who allowed the incompetence and ill-preparedness of his nation's defences to be humiliatingly exposed by China on the northern frontier? Better, perhaps, to have held his tongue and to have put his energies into effective domestic reforms and the rooting out of corruption. The list of criticisms could be extended almost at will.

But there is another side to be put. Nehru, quite simply, did his best. He attempted a policy of domestic reform that had some substantial, even spectacular, successes. Planning was placed at the centre of the Government's agenda, a pluralistic society was celebrated not denied, economic development was promoted, a genuine assault was made on underprivilege and poverty. All of this left India better off – both economically and morally – than under British rule.

As for external relations, it can plausibly be claimed that Nehru's achievements were considerable, even enviable. He made India the leader of the developing world through the power of his personality and the purity of his convictions. He thus gave a voice, even at second hand, to new nations struggling to make their mark in the international community. On his own terms he stood for justice, truth, and freedom. He encouraged the expression of an African identity, was instrumental in changing the nature of the Commonwealth, and contained the ambitions of both the west and the Soviet Union. The conflict with Pakistan was not of his making, and the Chinese Government deluded him with fair words while planning a war of aggression.

Above all, Nehru can be credited with the establishment of a strong democratic tradition in India, a tradition all the more honourable in contrast to the autocratic excesses of two near neighbours, both formerly under British rule, Pakistan and Burma. His commitment to the democratic process was genuine, and based upon shrewd calculation as well as upon personal and philosophical conviction. If sticking to democratic form resulted, far too often, in hiatus, inefficiency and failure, this was arguably but a small price to be paid in the long run.

There is, however, one final way of assessing Nehru's legacy. In the years since his death, India has witnessed the almost unbroken political domination of his descendants, first that of Indira Gandhi and then of her son, Rajiv Gandhi. A Nehru dynastic supremacy was, in practice, established on the back of India's democratic structure. This raises a host of awkward questions as to the nature of Indian democracy and the enduring power of political élites. It may, of course, simply reflect the enormous appeal of Nehru's image, the veneration felt towards the tradition which he established and the gratitude of the nation for his years of leadership. But there is a sting in the tail of this analysis. Both Indira Gandhi and Rajiv

Gandhi were killed by their political opponents. Assassination is hardly part of the democratic process. Although in this sense, Nehru's legacy may be judged one of failure rather than of success, it is also a sobering reminder of the enormous, and potentially destructive, task of ruling a country as large, complex, diverse and needy as India.

Notes

Notes to Chapter 1
[1] Sarvepalli Gopal, *Jawaharlal Nehru* (Oxford, 1989), p. 5.
[2] Quoted in M. J. Akbar, *Nehru : The Making of India*, (London, 1988), p. 48.
[3] Ibid, p. 53.
[4] *Selected Works of Jawaharlal Nehru*, vol. 1., ed. Rau, Prasad & Namda (Delhi, 1972) p. 39, 20 December 1907.
[5] S. Gopal, op. cit., p. 10.

Notes to Chapter 2
[1] S. Gopal, p. 104.
[2] J. Nehru, *The Independent*, 22 January 1921.

Notes to Chapter 3
[1] J. Nehru, *The Independent*, 25 May 1921.
[2] Quoted in S. Gopal, p. 34.
[3] *The Leader*, 14 July 1923.
[4] S. Gopal, p. 56.
[5] J. Nehru, *A Bunch of Old Letters*, (Delhi, 1958), p. 68.
[6] S. Gopal, p. 73.

Notes to Chapter 4
[1] Denis Judd, *Lord Reading*, (London, 1982), pp. 218–20.
[2] J. Nehru, Foreword to D. G. Tendulkar, *Mahatma*, vol. 1, (Delhi, 1951).
[3] M. Edwardes, *Nehru: A Political Biography* (Harmondsworth, 1971), p. 87.
[4] See J. Nehru, *An Autobiography*, (London, 1936).
[5] J. Nehru, Memorandum to National Planning Committee, 4 June 1939.

Notes to Chapter 5
[1] See J. Nehru, *The Unity of India*, (London, 1941), pp. 395–400.

² D. G. Tendulkar, *Mahatma*, vol. 6, p. 43.
³ *The Transfer of Power*, ed. Mansergh & Lumby, vol. 1, p. 598.
⁴ Ibid., vol. 1, pp. 726–30
⁵ Quoted in Edwardes, op. cit,. p. 144
⁶ Ibid., p. 148
⁷ J. Nehru, *The Discovery of India* (Calcutta, 1946).

Notes to Chapter 6

¹ R. J. Moore, *Escape from Empire* : *The Attlee Government and the Indian Problem* (Oxford, 1983), p. 31.
² Akbar, op. cit., p. 366.
³ Edwardes, op. cit., p. 169
⁴ *The Bombay Chronicle*, 8 July 1946

Notes to Chapter 7

¹ Philip Ziegler, *Mountbatten* : *the Official Biography*, (London, 1985), pp. 473–4; also Janet Morgan, *Edwina Mountbatten* : *a Life of Her Own* (London, 1991).
² Akbar, op. cit., p. 408.
³ Ibid.
⁴ Mansergh, N. & Moon, P., *The Transfer of Power*, vol. 10, pp. 756–7, London, 1981.
⁵ S. Gopal, op. cit., p. 175.
⁶ Broadcast, 30 January 1948, *Nehru's Speeches*, vol. 1, 1946–9, (New Delhi, 1949), pp. 42–4.

Notes to Chapter 8

¹ Speech of 2 October 1951, reported in *National Herald*, 4 October 1951.
² S. Gopal, op. cit., p. 185; Letter of Nehru to Sheikh Abdullah, 3 December 1947.
³ R. Beny, *India* (London, 1969), p. 189.
⁴ J. Nehru to B. N. Rau, 1 July 1950, quoted in Gopal, op. cit., p. 225.
⁵ Speech to Congress, *National Herald*, 14 October 1949.
⁶ M. Edwardes, op. cit., p. 274.

Notes to Chapter 9

¹ Speeches reported in *The Hindu*, 4 & 5 January 1957, and 13 May 1958.
² See A. H. Harrison, *The Process of Planning* : *A Study of India's Five Year Plans, 1950–64*, (Oxford, 1966).
³ Edwardes, op. cit., pp. 294–5.
⁴ Speech reported in *The Hindu*, 2 January 1961.
⁵ Edwardes, op. cit., p. 284.
⁶ Nehru's last will and testament, 21 June 1954, quoted in Akbar, op. cit., pp. 582–4.

Bibliography

Works by Nehru

An Autobiography, Lane, London, 1936.
India & the World, Allen & Unwin, London 1936.
Letters from a Father to a Daughter, Kitabistan, Allahabad, 1938.
Towards Freedom, John Day, New York, 1941.
The Discovery of India, Signet Press, Calcutta, 1946.
The Unity of India: collected writings, 1934–40, Drummond London, 1948.
A Bunch of Old Letters, Asia Publishing House, Bombay, 1958.
India's Foreign Policy, Government of India Publications Division, Delhi, 1961.
Selected Works of Jawaharlal Nehru (ed. Gopal, S.), Second series, vols. 1–15, NMML, New Delhi, 1984.
Nehru on Communalism (ed. Gupta, N. L.), SVC, Delhi, 1965.
Nehru's Letters to His Sister (ed. Hutheesingh, K.), Faber, London, 1963.
India's Independence and Social Revolution, Vikas, Delhi, 1984.
Letters to Chief Ministers, 1947–64 (ed. Parthasarathi), Oxford, 1985.
Selected Works of Jawaharlal Nehru (eds Rau, Prasad and Nandu), First series, vols. 1–5, Orient Longman, Delhi, 1972.
Two Alone, Two Together; letters between Indira Gandhi and Jawaharlal Nehru, 1940–64 (ed. Gandhi, Sonia), Hodder, London, 1992.

Biographical Studies of Nehru

Akbar, M. J., *Nehru: the Making of India*, Viking, London, 1988.

Brecher, Michael, *Nehru: a Political Biography*, OUP, Oxford, 1959.
Bright, J. S., *The Great Nehru*, Tagore Memorial Publications, Delhi, 1961.
Chand, Attar, *Jawaharlal Nehru: Arts, Culture, Literature & Languages*, H. K. Publishers, New Delhi, 1989.
Cousins, N. (ed.), *Profiles of Nehru*, Indian Book Company, Delhi, 1966.
Crocker, W. R., *Nehru*, London, Allen & Unwin, 1966.
Diawakar, R. R., *Nehru, and His Contribution to World Peace*, Gandhi Peace Foundation, New Delhi, 1989.
Edwardes, Michael, *Nehru: a Political Biography*, Penguin, Harmondsworth, 1971.
Gopal, S., *Jawaharlal Nehru: a biography*, 3 vols., Cape, London, 1976–84.
— *Jawaharlal Nehru: a biography* (abridged), OUP, Oxford, 1989.
Jawaharlal Nehru: a pictorial survey, Nehru Memorial Fund, Delhi, 1983.
Karaka, D. F., *Nehru: the Lotus Eater from Kashmir*, D. Verschoyle, Delhi, 1953.
Moraes, Francis R., *Jawaharlal Nehru: a Biography*, Macmillan, New York, 1956.
Mukherjee, H., *The Gentle Colossus: a study of Jawaharlal Nehru*, Manisha, Calcutta, 1964.
Nanda, B. R., *The Nehrus*, OUP, Oxford, 1984.
Rao, A., & B. G. Ras, *Six Thousand Days: Jawaharlal Nehru, Prime Minister*, Sterling, Delhi, 1974.
Raroof, A. A., *Nehru the Man*, Pearl Publications, Bombay, 1967.
Rau, M. C., *Jawaharlal Nehru*, Ministry of Information and Broadcasting, Delhi, 1973.
Seton, Marie, *Panditji: a Portrait of Jawaharlal Nehru*, Dobson, London, 1967.
Zakaria, Rafiq (ed.), *A Study of Nehru*, Rupa, Calcutta etc., 1989.

Other Books

Azad, A. K., *India Wins Freedom*, Orient Longman, Calcutta, 1959.
Bence-Jones, Mark, *The Viceroys of India*, Constable, London, 1982.
Beny, R., *India*, London, 1969.
Brown, Judith, *Modern India*, OUP, Oxford, 1985.
— *Gandhi*, Yale University Press, London, 1988.
Chakravarty, S., *Development Planning: the Indian Experience*, Clarendon Press, Oxford, 1987.
Chandra, B., *Communalism in Modern India*, Vikas, Delhi, 1984.

Desai, M., *Envoy to Nehru*, OUP, Oxford/Delhi, 1981.
Dutt, S., *With Nehru in the Foreign Office*, Minerva, Calcutta, 1977.
Frankel, F. R., *India's Political Economy, 1947–77*, Princeton University Press, New Jersey, 1978.
Gandhi, M. K., *An Autobiography, or My Experiment with Truth*, Cape, London, 1949.
Gopal, Ram, *Trials of Jawaharlal Nehru*, The Book Centre, Bombay, 1962.
Haksar, P. N. (ed.), *Nehru's Vision: Peace & Security in the Nuclear Age*, Patriot, Delhi, 1987.
Hangen, Welles, *After Nehru, Who?*, Hart-Davies, London, 1963.
Haq, Mushir A., *Muslim Politics in Modern India*, Meenakshi, Meerut, 1970.
Harrison, A. H., *The Process of Planning: a Study of India's Five Year Plans, 1950–64*, OUP, Oxford, 1966.
Hodson, H. V., *The Great Divide*, Hutchinson, London, 1969.
Jalal, Ayesha, *The Sole Spokesman: Jinnah, the Muslim League & the Demand for Pakistan*, CUP, Cambridge, 1985.
Judd, Denis, *Lord Reading*, Weidenfeld, London, 1982.
— *The British Raj*, Wayland, Brighton, 2nd edition, 1987.
Kalhan, Promilla, *Kamala Nehru: an Intimate Biography*, Vikas, Delhi, 1973.
Kamath, H. V., *The Last Days of Jawaharlal Nehru*, Jayasree Prakashan, Calcutta, 1977.
Karanjia, R. K., *The Philosophy of Mr. Nehru*, Allen & Unwin, London, 1966.
— *The Mind of Mr. Nehru*, Allen & Unwin, London, 1960.
Khera, S. S., *India's Defence Problem*, Orient Longman, Bombay, 1968.
Mansergh, N. & E. W. R. Lumby (eds.) vols. 1–4 and N. Mansergh and Penderel Moon (eds.) vols. 5–9, *The Transfer of Power*, HMSO, London, 1981.
Mathai, M. O., *My Days With Nehru*, Vikas, Delhi, 1979.
Misra, B. B., *The Indian Political Parties*, OUP, Delhi, 1976.
Moore, R. J., *The Crisis of Indian Unity*, OUP, Oxford & Delhi, 1974.
— *Escape from Empire: the Attlee Government and the Indian Problem*, Clarendon Press, Oxford, 1983.
— *Making the New Commonwealth*, Clarendon Press, Oxford, 1987.
Morgan, Janet, *Edwina Mountbatten: a Life of Her Own*, Harper Collins, London, 1991.
Morgan, Kenneth O., *Labour in Power, 1945–51*, OUP, Oxford, 1984.

Nanda, B. R. (ed.), *Indian Foreign Policy: the Nehru Years*, Vikas, Delhi, 1976.
Philips, C. H. (ed.), *The Evolution of India & Pakistan, 1858–1947*, Select Documents, OUP, Oxford, 1962.
Prasad, Rajendra, *India Divided*, Anmol Publications, Delhi, 1986.
Reid, Escott, *Envoy to Nehru*, OUP, Oxford, 1981.
Robinson, Francis, *Separatism Among Indian Muslims: the Politics of the United Provinces' Muslims, 1860–1923*, CUP, Cambridge, 1974.
Singh, Anita Inder, *The Origins of the Partition of India, 1936–47*, OUP, Delhi, 1987.
Singh, Charan, *India's Economic Policy*, Vikas, Delhi, 1978.
Singh, K. N. (ed.) *Legacy of Nehru*, Vikas, Delhi, 1984.
Tendulkar, D. G., *Mahatma: The Life of Mohandas Karamchand Gandhi*, 8 vols., Government of India Publications, Delhi, 1951.
Wavell, Lord (ed. P. Moon), *The Viceroy's Journal*, OUP, Oxford, 1973.
Wolpert, Stanley, *Jinnah of Pakistan*, OUP, New York, 1984.
Ziegler, Philip, *Mountbatten: the official biography*, Collins, London, 1985.

Index

Abdullah, Sheikh, 47
Africanism, 66, 85
Ahmadnagar Fort, 38
Ahmedabad, 73
Akali Dahl movement, 14
Aksai Chin, 77, 78
Alexander, A. V., 45
All India Congress Committee, 14, 38, 43, 80
Allahabad, 1, 2, 3, 7, 10, 12, 14, 25, 82
Allahabad municipal board, 15
Ambedkar, Dr, 26
Amery, Leopold, 33, 37
Amritsar, massacre at, 9
apartheid, 79, 84
Asian–African Conference, Bandung 1955, 52, 66
Asian Relations Conference, New Delhi 1947, 51–2
Asianism, 51, 66
Assam, 72
Atlantic Charter, 35–6
Attlee, Clement, 18, 41, 42, 45, 48–9
Autobiography, 26
Avadh (Oudh), 10
Ayub Khan, Mohammed, 79
Azad, A. K., 36, 37

Bandung Conference 1955, 52, 66
Bengal, 4, 44, 52, 53, 54
Besant, Annie, 8
Bevan, Aneurin, 42
Bevin, Ernest, 42
Bhutan, 77
Bihar, 73
Bombay, 25, 45, 65, 73
Bose, Subhas, 26, 28, 34, 39, 43
British Commonwealth of Nations, 2, 30, 36, 45, 61, 66, 79, 85
British Conservative party, 20, 24, 40
British Government
  Labour administration 1929–31, 21 (*see also* Round Table Conferences)
  Cripps mission 1942, 35–7

Labour administration 1945–51, 41, 42–3, 45–9
and modernization of India's army 1962, 78
(*see also* Simon Commission)
British Labour party, 84
British Raj
  in 1919, 8–9
  steps towards transfer of power in India up to 1930, 20–2
  Gandhi–Irwin pact, 22–4
  repression 1932, 25
  and Second World War, 31–9
  new negotiations with nationalists 1945, 40
  (*see also* partition of India)
Brooks, F. T., 3

Cabinet Mission 1946, 45–7
Calcutta, 45, 47, 53
Cambridge University, 4–6, 84
capitalism, 16, 83
caste system, 2, 61, 63
Chelmsford, Lord, 8
China, 29, 60, 66, 67, 75, 76–8, 85
Chou Enlai, 77
Churchill, Sir Winston, 20, 22, 32, 33, 35, 36, 37, 40, 41
civil disobedience *see satyagraha*
civil rights, 60–1, 63–4
Cold War, 65, 67
colonialism *see* imperialism
communism, 16, 17, 18, 26, 66, 68, 72, 76
Community Development Programme, 2, 63, 70
Congo, 79
Constituent Assembly, 48, 53, 60
constitution of India, 60–1, 63, 64, 74
corruption, 55, 67, 71, 85
Cripps, Sir Stafford, 35–7, 42, 45
Curzon, Lord, 4

Dalai Lama, 77

INDEX

Dandi, 21
Dawn, 32
Dehra Dun, 33, 81
Delhi, 14, 44
democracy, 31, 70, 84, 85–6
demonstrations, 9, 10–11, 13, 18, 21 (*see also* mutinies; riots)
developing countries, 51–2, 84, 85 (*see also* imperialism)
Discovery of India, The, 39–40
dominion status, 17, 18, 36, 53, 61
Dyer, Brigadier-General, 9

elections
  1936–7, 27
  1945, 43–4
  1952, 61
  1957, 71, 72, 73
  1962, 75–6

fascism, 25–6, 28, 31, 84
Federal Court, 61
federation, Government of India Act 1935 and, 27
Five Year Plans, 2, 62–3, 69, 70–1, 83
Franco, General, 28

Gandhi, Mrs Indira, 7, 16, 26, 32, 34, 52, 80, 81, 85–6
Gandhi, Mahatma (M. K.), 1, 81
  before 1930, 8, 9, 10, 13, 14, 15, 17, 18, 20
  in 1930s, 21, 22–5, 26, 27, 28
  in 1939–45, 31, 32–3, 35, 36, 37, 38–9, 40
  partition of India and death, 55–6, 57, 59
  (*see also* non-violence; *satyagraha*)
Gandhi, Rajiv, 85–6
Gandhi, Sanjay, 81
Ganges, 81–2
Goa, 58, 66, 75
Gokhale, G. K., 4
Government of India Act 1919, 8
Government of India Act 1935, 26–7, 60
Great Britain *see* British
Great Depression, 25
Gujarat, Gujaratis, 65, 73
Gurkhas, 21

Harrow School, 3–4, 84
Himalayas, 81, 82
Hindu Code, 2, 64
Hindu Marriage Act 1956, 64
Hindu Succession Act 1955, 64

Hitler, Adolf, 25, 28, 31
Home Rule Leagues, 8
Hungarian uprising, 66
Hyderabad, 52, 54, 58–9

Imperial Conference 1926, 17
imperialism, 16, 28, 66, 67, 84
Independence for India League, 17, 18
Independent, The, 8, 10, 12
Indian Army, 20, 21, 72
Indian Civil Service, 5, 20, 21
Indian National Army, 39, 43–4, 50
Indian National Congress, 1
  early years, 3, 4, 8
  1920s, 12, 13, 14, 16, 18
  1930s, 22–9
  1939–45, 31–40
  1945–7, 43–8
  1947–8, 53, 54
  1948–64, 57–8, 60, 61, 67, 71, 72, 73, 75–6, 80
  National Planning Committee, 29, 33
  interim government 1946–7, 47–8
International Congress against Colonial Oppression and Imperialism 1927, 16
internationalism, 2, 51, 59, 66, 79–80, 85 (*see also* non-alignment)
Irish nationalism, 4–5
Irwin, Lord, 22–4

Jabalpur, 73
Jan Sangh party, 76
Japan, 25, 28, 34, 35–6, 37, 38, 39
Jinnah, Mohammed Ali, 27, 31, 32, 37, 40, 43, 44, 46, 47, 48, 52, 53
Johnson, Colonel, 37
Junagadh, 54, 58, 59

Kamaraj, K., 80
Karachi, 24, 45
Kashmir, 2, 41, 52, 81
  incorporation into India, 47, 54, 58, 59–60, 79, 84
Kaul, Kamala *see* Nehru, Kamala
Kennedy, President J. F., 80
Kerala, 72, 84
Khilafat movement, 12
Khrushchev, Nikita, 80
Korean War, 65, 67

Lahore, 18, 53

language
  linguistic provinces, 64–5, 68, 73
  national, 65, 73–4
  use of Urdu, 74
Laski, Harold, 42, 84
League against Imperialism and for National Independence, 16
Lenin, V. I. U., 15, 17
linguistic provinces, 64–5, 68, 73
Lucknow, 13, 18

MacDonald, Ramsay, 21, 24
McMahon line, 77
Madhya Pradesh, 73
Madras, 45
Maharashtra, 65, 73
Marxism, 16, 17
Menon, Krishna, 52, 76
Montagu–Chelmsford reforms, 8–9
Moore, R. J., 42
Morley–Minto reforms, 8
Morris, William, 5
Morrison, Herbert, 42
Mountbatten, Edwina, Lady, 2, 50, 51, 52
Mountbatten of Burma, Louis Mountbatten, 1st Earl, 49, 50–4, 55, 58, 59, 84
Munich Agreement, 28
Muslim League, 27, 31, 32, 36, 39, 40, 43, 44–5, 46, 47–8, 52, 53
Muslims, 2, 73, 74
  Khilafat movement, 12
  and partition *see* Muslim League
  women, 64, 83
  (*see also* princely states)
Mussoorie, 22, 34
Mussolini, B., 15
mutinies of 1946, 45 (*see also* demonstrations; riots)

Nabha, 14
Nagas, 72–3, 84
Namboodiripad, E. M. S., 72
National Conference, 47
National Planning Commission, 62, 71
nationalization, 17, 62
Nehru, Indira *see* Gandhi, Mrs Indira
Nehru, Jawaharlal
  (1889–1912) birth and early life, 2–3, education, 3–6, 84
  (1912–21) marriage, 7–8, joins Home Rule League, 8, and development of nationalism after Amritsar, 9–11

  (1920s) arrested, 13–14, resigns from AICC and UP provincial Congress committees, 14, personal troubles, 15, chairman of Allahabad municipal board, 15, visits Europe, 16–17, commitment to independence and socialism, 17–18, 19, demonstrates against Simon Commission, 18, elected to presidency of Indian National Congress, 18–19
  (1930s) imprisonment 1930, 21–2, forbidden to address public meetings and rearrested Oct. 1930, 22, and Irwin–Gandhi pact 22–4, arrest and imprisonment 1931, 25, personal difficulties, 26, publishes *Autobiography*, 26, elected President of Congress for 1936, 26, election of 1936–7, 27, visits Europe, 26, 28, 42, campaign against Subhas Bose, 28, visits China, 29
  (1939–45) attitude to Second World War, 31, arrest and imprisonment Oct. 1940, 33–4, release 1941 and reaction to Japanese advance, 34–5, and Cripps's constitutional initiative, 35–8, imprisonment 1942, 38, 39–40, *The Discovery of India*, 39–40
  (1945–7) and Indian National Army, 43–4, Cabinet Mission, 45–7, and Indian princes, 47, heads interim government 1946, 47–8, 57
  (1947–8) relations with Mountbatten, 50–1, and Asian Relations Conference, 51, reaction to Mountbatten's partition plan, 52–3, speech 3 June 1947, 53–4, speech 14 Aug. 1947, 54, Prime Minister of independent India, 55–6
  (1948–64) rivalry with Sardar V. Patel, 57–8, deals with princely states and Kashmir, 58–60, 79, social and economic policy, 61–4, 67–71, 83–4, 85, educational policy, 64, and linguistic provinces, 64–5, 68, 73, and national language, 65, 73–4, foreign and international policy, 2, 65–7, 69, 70, 75, 76–80, 84–5, domestic power and difficulties, 67–8, 71–4, incorporation of Goa into Union, 74–5, failing health and death, 76, 80–2

criticisms of, 83–5, financial difficulties, 6, founder of dynasty, 2, 85–6, as lawyer, 5–6, 7, 15, 44, relationship with Gandhi, 10, 13, 17, 23, 26, 35, 55–6, summary of achievements, 1–2, 85, Western influence on, 1, 4–5, 6, 16–17, 84
Nehru, Kamala, 7–8, 15, 16, 22, 26
Nehru, Motilal, 1, 3–4, 5, 6, 7, 10, 13, 15, 16, 17, 18, 21, 22, 23
Nehru Report 1928, 18
Nepal, 77
New Delhi, 36, 51, 81
non-alignment, 2, 65–7, 69, 70, 75, 78–9, 84, 85
non-cooperation, 10, 12–13, 14–15, 19, 20, 27, 31–2, 34
(*see also satyagraha*)
non-violence, 11, 33, 34, 55, 66, 75
North West Frontier Province, 44, 53, 54

Official Languages Act 1963, 74

Pakistan, 43, 44, 45–6, 52, 54, 58, 59, 78, 84, 85
panchayats (village committees), 11, 67
Parliament, 60, 67, 80
partition
  of Bengal 1905, 4
  of India, 27, 32, 36, 44–7, 52–5
Partition Committee, 54
Patel, Vallabhbhai, 57–8
Pathans, 59
Pethick-Lawrence, Lord, 45
pluralism, 67, 73, 83, 85
Portugal, 58, 66, 74–5
Pratapgarh, 10
Preventive Detention Act, 73
princes, princely states, 22, 27, 36, 47, 48, 53, 54, 58–60
Punjab, 14, 44, 52, 53, 54, 65

racialism, 66 (*see also* apartheid)
Rau, B. N., 65
Reading, Lord, 21
republicanism, 19, 61
riots, 38–9, 47, 48, 53, 55, 72, 73 (*see also* demonstrations; mutinies)
Roosevelt, President, 35, 37
Round Table Conferences, 22–4, 26
Rowlatt Acts, 9

Royal Commission on Indianisation, 21
Russia *see* Soviet Union

salt monopoly, 21, 23
satyagraha ('truth force'; often associated with civil disobedience), 1, 9, 10, 13, 19, 20, 21, 22, 25, 32–3, 38 (*see also* non-cooperation)
Second World War, 30–41
  social and economic effects on India, 34, 40
secularism, 60, 73
Shastri, Lal Bahadur, 75, 80, 81
Sikhs, 14, 53, 65
Simla, 40, 46, 52
Simon Commission, 18, 20, 21
Sind, 44
Singh, Baldev, 53
Sinn Fein, 5
socialism, 1, 11, 16, 17–18, 19, 24, 25–6, 28, 29, 61, 62, 63, 70, 71, 83, 84
South Africa, 79, 84
Soviet Union, 1, 16–17, 70, 75, 78, 85
Srinagar, 59
Statute of Westminster 1931, 30
Suez crisis, 66, 67, 79, 84
Suhrawardy, Hussein Shaheed, 47
swadeshi, 12
Swatantra party, 76

Tandon, P. D., 58
Tata, 15
theosophy, 3, 8
Tibet, 76–8
Tilak, B. G., 8

United Nations, 59, 65, 66, 84
United Provinces, 2, 8, 10–11, 12, 17 (*see also* Allahabad)
United States, 67, 75, 78, 79, 84
universal suffrage, 60
untouchability, 2, 24, 26, 61, 63, 83
Uttar Pradesh, 73 (*see also* Allahabad)

Vietnam War, 79

Wavell, Lord, 37, 40, 42, 47, 48, 49
Willingdon, Lord, 24, 25, 31, 32, 37
women, 63–4, 83
Women's Army Corps, 40
World Bank, 69

World War II *see* Second World War

Yeravda, 22

zamindari system, 10, 17, 63

The Author

Professor Denis Judd teaches Commonwealth, Imperial and South Asian History at the University of North London, where he is Subject Leader of the South Asian Studies degree programme. He took his first degree at Oxford, his Ph.D. at London, and is a Fellow of the Royal Historical Society. Among his books are *Balfour and the British Empire* (1968), *The Victorian Empire* (1970), *Lord Palmerston* (1975), *The Boer War* (1977), *Radical Joe; a Life of Joseph Chamberlain* (1977), *Lord Reading* (1982), *The Evolution of the Modern Commonwealth* (with Peter Slinn) (1982), *The British Raj* (new edition 1987) and a number of other biographical and historical studies. He has written documentary programmes for BBC Radio 4, a variety of articles and contributions to books, and has reviewed extensively in the national press and in academic journals. He was born in Northamptonshire and now lives in north-west London. He is married and has four children.

The General Editor

Professor Kenneth O. Morgan, D.Litt, FBA, is Principal of the University of Wales, Aberystwyth and pro-Vice-Chancellor, and was formerly Fellow and Praelector of The Queen's College, Oxford. He has written extensively on nineteenth-century and twentieth-century Britain; his titles include *Wales in British Politics, 1868–1922* (1963), *The Age of Lloyd George* (1971), *Keir Hardie* (1975), *Consensus and Disunity* (1979), *Rebirth of a Nation: Wales 1880–1980* (1981), *Labour in Power 1945–1951* (1984), *Labour People* (1987) and *The People's Peace: British History, 1945–1989* (1990). He has been editor of *The Welsh History Review* since 1965 and was elected Fellow of the British Academy in 1983. He is currently writing the official biography of Lord Callaghan.